EVEREST
A TREKKER'S GUIDE

Distant view of Everest from Gokyo Ri (5340m: 17,520ft). (p133)

EVEREST
A TREKKER'S GUIDE

by

Kev Reynolds

CICERONE PRESS
MILNTHORPE, CUMBRIA, UK

ISBN 1 85284 187 7
A catalogue record for this book is available from the British Library

ACKNOWLEDGEMENTS

As ever, I am grateful to Alan Payne, trekking and climbing partner of many years, who shared long weeks in the Khumbu, echoed my enthusiasm for mountains, valleys and villages along the way, and patiently accepted delays and diversions in the name of research. His company adds to the experience. Roland Hiss provided much welcome advice as a result of his long experience of the Everest regions of both Nepal and Tibet, and gave me access to some of his photographs of the mountain from the north. I thank him for his input. Other trekkers added to pleasures along the trail, especially Denis and Danielle from Canada, Alain, Noelle, Lionel and Isobelle from France, along with numerous lodge owners and all the smiling Nepali people who brightened each day with their laughing eyes and greetings of *Namaste*. Thanks to Tendi Sherpa and Dawa Tshiring Sherpa; the first for valuable route information, the second for organising flights out of Lukla within a remarkably short space of time. In Kathmandu, Keshav Karki, of Manakamana River Adventure, acted as our agent and helped reduce some of the bureaucratic hassles. My publishers are thanked for their continued support over the years, and for providing me with the perfect excuse once more to go trekking in Nepal. Finally, the debt to my wife grows as yet again she stayed behind to pay the bills and keep the home together while I wandered among the mountains and enjoyed another 'hard day at the office'. No-one could hope for better or more loving support than she so willingly gives.

Kev Reynolds

Cicerone Guides by the same author:

Annapurna - a Trekker's Guide	*Walks in the Engadine - Switzerland*
Walks & Climbs in the Pyrenees	*The Valais*
The Wealdway & The Vanguard Way	*The Jura (with R. B. Evans)*
Walking in Kent Vols I & II	*The Bernese Alps*
The South Downs Way & The Downs Link	*Ticino*
The Cotswold Way	*Central Switzerland*
Chamonix to Zermatt - the Walker's Haute Route	*Alpine Pass Route*

Forthcoming:
Langtang, Gosainkund & Helambu - a Trekker's Guide

Front Cover: Kusum Kangguru towers over the Dudh Kosi valley - seen from the trail below Manidingma. (p81)

CONTENTS

ADVICE TO READERS

Readers are advised that whilst every effort is taken by the author to ensure the accuracy of this guidebook, changes can occur which may affect the contents. It is advisable to check locally on transport, accommodation, shops, etc. but even rights of way can be altered and, more especially overseas, paths can be eradicated by landslip, forest fires or changes of ownership.

    The publisher would welcome notes of any such changes.

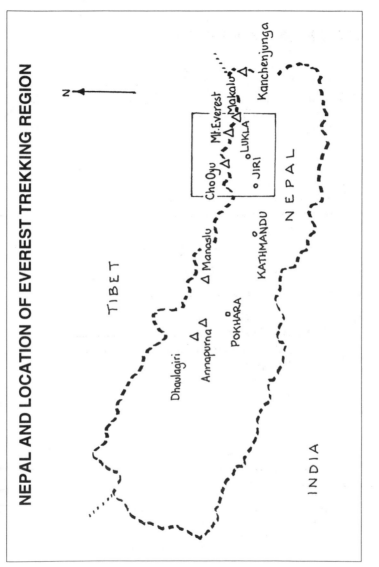

NEPAL AND LOCATION OF EVEREST TREKKING REGION

N

TIBET

Dhaulagiri

△ Annapurna △

o POKHARA

△ Manaslu

△ Cho Oyu △ Mt.Everest
△ Makalu
o LUKLA △
o JIRI
Kanchenjunga

o KATHMANDU

N E P A L

I N D I A

REGION OF EVEREST TREKS

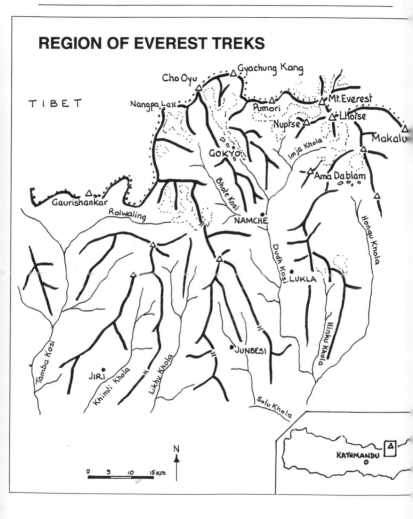

PREFACE

The Himalayan Kingdom of Nepal is a trekker's dream world. The dramatic beauty of its mountains is legendary, its people among the most warm-hearted, gentle and openly friendly that you could possibly wish to meet. From the lush foothills stepped with immaculate terracing, to the stark upper regions of snow, ice and towering walls of rock, a series of unfolding landscapes impress all who wander through. None who are lured along its trails need fear disappointment.

This book is a guide to just one region of this magical land - the district inhabited by the Sherpa and known as Solu-Khumbu. Among its sparkling mountains Cho Oyu, Ama Dablam, Kangtega, Thamserku, Nuptse and Lhotse each present powerful images, as do many others with less familiar names. But it is Mount Everest that naturally provides the magnet for the vast majority of trekkers and all who love the high, wild places.

Traditionally known among both Khumbu Sherpas and Tibetans to the north as Chomolungma, 'Goddess Mother of the World', the highest mountain on Earth has more recently been given the official name of Sagarmatha by the Government of Nepal. Throughout this guidebook, however, the more widely known appellation of Everest is used. Adopted by the West as long ago as 1865, it is this name by which the mountain is more widely known and instantly recognised today.

Each of the trekking routes described in the following pages will open the eyes of the sensitive traveller to scenes of unbelievable grandeur. Whether your plan is to study Mount Everest in some detail from the crown of Kala Pattar, or to gaze at it from Thyangboche's rhododendron-clad slopes; whether you aim to explore the lake-gemmed delights of Gokyo or the raw beauties of the valley of the Imja Khola below the huge wall of Lhotse, rewards will be plentiful.

Trekking through Solu-Khumbu also provides an opportunity to build a relationship with people of a different culture, a vastly different background, a different outlook on life; people who seem largely content and unencumbered by possessions, who live free from the drive of competition, and among whom the passage of time has an entirely different meaning to ours. The strong Buddhist faith of the Sherpas has manifested itself not only in the way they live, but also in the landscapes in which they live; nature, environment and human activity balanced by the pivot of this faith. We, as trekkers from an alien culture, need to be aware of that balance and determine not to upset it.

How you interact with both the country and its inhabitants will depend on the degree of sensitivity carried with you. The riches you harvest will be measured by your willingness, or otherwise, to put Western values in abeyance and to submit yourself to the multiplicity of experiences available and waiting there. Trekking in the shadow of Mount Everest can be a feast. There's no need to go on a diet.

Trail information contained in this book reflects as accurately as possible the routes as found during research. However, each monsoon adds its own signature to the landscape. Trails and bridges may be washed away and replaced elsewhere. Villages expand, tea-houses and lodges multiply, and paths are re-routed when landslips reshape a hillside. In order to improve and update future editions of this guide, I'd appreciate the assistance of readers who could provide a note of changes found on trek. I would also welcome comments or suggestions that might be beneficial to trekkers in the future. All notes and corrections sent to me via the publisher will be gratefully received.

It should be borne in mind that heights and distances quoted may not be entirely accurate. Different maps give varying figures and widely disparate spellings for some of the villages, mountains and passes. None of this should matter too much, for most of the names at least should be fairly obvious, and heights and distances are given merely to serve as a rough guide. Times quoted for the various stages on trek are likewise estimates only, but are offered as an indication of the length of each day's walk. They do not allow for tea-house delays nor photographic interruptions (and there'll be plenty of these), but are based on actual walking time. I have attempted to be consistent throughout, but variations are bound to creep in over the course of several weeks' trekking. My advice is to use these times as a loose guide, not as a challenge.

Introduction

Mountains are fountains, not only of rivers and fertile soil, but of men. Therefore we are all, in some sense, mountaineers, and going to the mountains is going home. (John Muir)

For all its great bulk and a height of 8848m (29,028ft) Mount Everest is remarkably shy and for many days successfully eludes the gaze of trekkers approaching from the south. On the walk-in from Jiri there is one memorable stretch of trail between Junbesi and Sallung where for a few glorious minutes an amazing line of snowpeaks, including Everest, marks the far horizon. Then it's gone, not to appear again for several days until a bend on the final slope leading to Namche Bazaar grants but a brief, tantalising glimpse.

Beyond Namche, however, the summit pyramid, often devoid of snow, appears from a variety of viewpoints as a black crown perched on the Nuptse-Lhotse ridge. All around other peaks, of varying altitudes and degrees of grandeur, jostle for attention while Everest impresses, as has been said, not so much by its great height, 'but by the suggestion...of the immensity of its unseen mass'.

For most trekkers following the trails in this book a clear view of the world's highest mountain will be the lure. That is understandable. But Everest is merely one among dozens of stunning peaks that crowd each day in Khumbu. Stand on the summit of Gokyo Ri and a truly remarkable panorama displays rank upon rank of snow, ice and rock peak, each carved with its own savage profile, while far below shines a turquoise lake and beyond its walling moraine the longest glacier in Nepal stretches grey, bleak and rubble-strewn.

At the head of Gokyo's valley, Cho Oyu, one of the first 'eight thousanders' ever to be climbed, presents an almost featureless white face, a vast wall of snow-covered ice, while neighbouring Gyachung Kang provides a neatly sculpted contrast, appealing yet formidable with its bare-rock buttresses rising steeply from the glaciers.

Then there are the ice-crusted walls and pinnacles of Kangtega and Thamserku soaring above Namche, and nearby Ama Dablam, as

11

easily recognised and as eternally memorable as Machhapuchhare (the 'fish-tail' peak in the Annapurna Himal). From the trail above Namche, as from Khumjung and Thyangboche, graceful Ama Dablam dominates views along the valley of the Imja Khola. Yet if you trek farther upvalley and view it from the north, the mountain is transformed entirely, yet still it remains handsome, aloof and seemingly unattainable.

And from Kala Pattar below the stately Pumori, directly opposite Everest itself, the impressive west flank of Nuptse with its fluted peak, its great daubs of meringue-like snow and hanging glaciers, shames its more illustrious neighbour with startling beauty. If ever there were a crystal mountain Nuptse, seen from this view, would be it.

These, and other magnificent peaks, provide all the visual drama for which Nepal is so justly famed.

Nepal claims eight of the ten highest mountains in the world. Of these, three are Khumbu mountains (Everest, Lhotse and Cho Oyu), while a fourth (Makalu) is seen from specific viewpoints on and above the trail. Not without good reason did the much travelled Bill Tilman call this 'the grandest thirty miles of the Himalaya'.

Yet trekking in Solu-Khumbu is more than a simple adoration of mountains, for there are other aspects of the region that will enhance the whole experience of travel there. Villages along the trail, for example, reflect a way of life long forgotten by the developed world. Men and women still work the land either with the aid of water buffalo (in the foothills), or simply by hand (in the higher regions). As there are no roads there are no wheeled vehicles and all goods must be transported on the backs of porters or by strings of ponies or yaks. Along the trail prayer flags, prayer wheels, mani walls, chortens, stupas and gold-topped gompas all symbolise a tranquillity of spirit ignored by our industrialised society.

For many, trekking in the Khumbu can become almost a spiritual experience, a communion with both nature and man. Along the trails described in the following pages one has an opportunity to touch heaven every day.

EVEREST AND THE SOLU-KHUMBU REGION

The pull of Everest was stronger for me than any force on earth.
(Tenzing Norgay)

Tucked away among a bevy of huge mountains in north-eastern Nepal, Mount Everest forms a pyramid with three great ridges, along two of which runs the border with Tibet. The southerly of these drops to the South Col, then rises to the summit of Lhotse (8501m: 27,890ft), from which other ridges splay out both to west and east. An enormous horseshoe, known as the Western Cwm, is created by the linking of Everest, Lhotse and Nuptse, and out of this cascades the Khumbu glacier.

It is the river which springs from this glacier, and other tributary glaciers feeding into it, that waters the Solu-Khumbu region on its tumultuous journey south - out through the middle hills and foothills of Nepal, out to the steamy, low-lying Terai and the Gangetic plain of India.

Khumbu is the mountainous Sherpa-inhabited region fanning southward from Mount Everest to the junction of the Bhote Kosi and Dudh Kosi rivers below Namche Bazaar; Solu, the middle hills that drain into the Solu Khola west of the Dudh Kosi. Linking the Solu district with that of Khumbu is the region known as Pharak - 'the area that connects'.

South of the Nuptse-Lhotse wall a tributary valley joins that of the Khumbu just below Pheriche, bringing with it the meltwater of numerous glaciers, three of which form an icy moat round the trekking peak of Imja Tse, more descriptively known as Island Peak.

Below the junction of these two valleys the river flows south-westward and is known as the Imja Khola, but it soon trades this name for the Dudh Kosi at Thyangboche. Here another major tributary flows down from the frontier mountains - the Dudh Kosi, born in the Ngozumpa glacier projecting through the Gokyo valley from Cho Oyo and a host of stunning peaks.

Once the Dudh Kosi and Imja Khola rivers merge the valley narrows with huge walls rising on either side, and south of Namche Bazaar it becomes a veritable gorge. Then the Bhote Kosi swells the Dudh Kosi immediately below Namche, having drained more frontier mountains on the ridge continuing west of Cho Oyu. At the head of the Bhote Kosi's valley lies the Nangpa La, a pass traditionally used by generations of Tibetans for cross-border trade with the Sherpas of Khumbu, while above Thame, the main village in the valley, the pass of Trashi Labtsa provides a regular, though potentially dangerous, route into Rolwaling.

The Dudh Kosi gorge begins to open out at Mondzo, a trail-side village on the edge of the Sagarmatha National Park. Some 1200 square kilometres (463 square miles) of mountainous country north of Mondzo, in effect all of Khumbu except the villages which are excluded from its authority, were incorporated into the National Park in 1976, and the Park was declared a World Heritage Site three years later.

South of Mondzo the Dudh Kosi ploughs a long straight furrow and its valley remains quite narrow, squeezed in places by mountain spurs pushing from either side, and only on rare occasions is it flat-bedded and broad enough to encourage villagers to turn its banks to agriculture. From Kharikhola down, though, the hillsides have been immaculately terraced and a variety of crops respond to the lower altitudes and a benevolent climate.

All the main river valleys hereabouts run roughly southward between long foothill (or middle hill) ridges, several of which are connected by ancient passes. West of the Dudh Kosi the Beni Khola joins the Junbesi Khola above Phaplu to become the Solu Khola. The headwaters of the first of these rise in the snow and glaciers of Numbur and Khatang, then flow between pine-clad hills and orchards of apples, peaches and apricots. From the ridge crests, as from Sallung, long views north show an immaculate row of white teeth etched upon the horizon - Khumbu peaks rising over a succession of intervening ridges.

This is Solu-Khumbu, a magical land full of charm and grace; a trekker's dream world.

TREKKING AND TREKKING STYLES

The art of Himalayan travel...is the art of being bold enough to enjoy life now. (W.H. Murray)

Trekking is the simplest way to travel - on foot; a journey through an unfamiliar land, moving on day after day as though on pilgrimage. And in common with the pilgrim those who gain most from it are they who have managed to cast off the anxieties that beset their everyday life, who readily absorb each new experience, and who live in every moment of the present.

Wandering the trails of Nepal can be, and should be, a life-enriching experience. Since the rate of progress through each day is self-governing, opportunities abound for observing the intricacies of the trail, of fellow travellers (trekkers, porters and local Nepalis about their daily business); flowers, trees and shrubs; animals, birds and butterflies; village life; the changing light on a distant mountain; the roar of a river, tinkle of a yak bell, the welcoming call of *Namaste*. There are scents, too, to draw upon. In the foothills they're often heavy with sun-drenched vegetation, while at altitude the crisp fragrance of morning is a tonic that sharpens all the senses. There's the taste of dust that fills the air after a yak train has passed by; the smell of woodsmoke drifting over the rooftops of Sherpa houses; or the more acrid, eye-smarting effects of a yak-dung fire in a remote trekker's lodge.

Although you'll turn your back on most of the trappings of Western society, trekking towards Everest, though far from any road, could not be considered a true wilderness experience for there are many villages or hamlets liberally spaced along the valleys described in this guide, and a tourist infrastructure has developed which caters to the needs of thousands of visitors who annually flock there. This infrastructure enables a choice of trekking styles to be enjoyed.

There are several different ways to trek in Nepal. There's the organised variety where a group of people travel under the auspices of a commercial trekking agent (adventure travel company). There's independent trekking, where two or three friends forsake the company of porters or guides, travel light and use tea-houses and lodges throughout - sometimes referred to as 'tea-house trekking'. And there's a third course, a cross between independent and group travel, when a porter-guide is employed both to carry the trekker's gear and to lead him along the trail using lodges for overnight accommodation. Few regions of the Himalaya provide better facilities to accommodate trekkers of all persuasions than does that of Solu-Khumbu.

The particular style to suit each individual will depend upon such considerations as cost, personal experience of mountain travel, availability of like-minded friends with whom to undertake the journey, amount of time required to organise and carry out the trek, choice of route to follow, etc. The following paragraphs, written with particular regard to the Everest region, may help you decide which option is most appropriate for you.

Trekking with an Adventure Travel Company:

This is the obvious choice for those with more money than time, who dislike the hassles of organisation, who get frustrated with bureaucracy, or who have limited mountain experience and want a degree of security. Trekking with a reputable adventure travel company does away with all pre-departure worries and trek concerns. Read the brochures and all dossiers carefully, sign the form, make out your cheque and let someone else take care of the arrangements. One of the most important things you are paying for is expertise.

A product of this expertise is pre-departure advice with regard to inoculations, visa requirements and a suggested kit list. All flights to and from Kathmandu, and transfers and other travel arrangements within Nepal will be taken care of, as will hotel accommodation and the provision of trekking permits. Some companies also hire out items of equipment that would otherwise be rather expensive to buy, like a good-quality sleeping bag or a duvet suitable for wear at high altitudes.

On a group trek in Solu-Khumbu porters or yaks carry all camping equipment, food, kitchen stores and personal baggage, leaving the trekker free to shoulder just a light rucksack containing a few items likely to be required during the day, such as water bottle, spare film, pullover or duvet.

Nights are usually spent in tents. All meals are prepared and served by a staff of trained Nepalese cooks and kitchen boys; latrines are dug by the trek crew, tents erected and dismantled for you, and

Sherpa guides ensure that you do not get lost along the trail. A sirdar takes overall responsibility for the smooth running of the trek, but usually a Western leader also accompanies the group to liaise between trekkers and local staff. This leader often has an understanding of any medical problems likely to be encountered, and is in charge of a comprehensive first aid kit. Some companies based in the UK offer financial incentives to qualified medical personnel who accompany groups on a particular route.

It's a very sociable way to travel. Daily you will be walking, and sharing experiences, with people you may never have met before, and lasting relationships sometimes develop from on-trek introductions. Conversely, you may find it difficult to get on with another member of the group, in which case a degree of tact may need to be exercised to avoid a clash of personalities. On the whole groups are usually of a sufficient size (10-14 is normal) to make it possible to steer clear of anyone whose personality rubs against your own, without it becoming too obvious. Friction within a group is rare, and when it does occur it is usually short-lived.

Organised parties, of course, generally need to keep to a predetermined route and maintain a fairly strict schedule, which can be a little frustrating if you pass an enticing side glen you'd like to visit. On the other hand, since each day's stage is limited by the distance a laden porter can cover, the journey is made at a leisurely pace, thus allowing plenty of time to enjoy the scenery, visit an occasional monastery, study the flowers or indulge in photography along the trail.

The group trekker's day begins with a mug of tea being thrust through the tent flap at around 6.00am, closely followed by a bowl of hot water for washing. Breakfast is served soon after. In the foothills this will be eaten outdoors with views of distant mountains and hills warming to the new day. In higher, colder country, a mess tent will be used.

The day's walk starts early, around 7.30am when the light is pure, the air cool and birds active. The trek crew will break camp as porters pack their dokos (large conical baskets in which goods are carried) and set off along the trail. During the morning's walk the kitchen crew will rattle past and select a lunch spot, often with a fine view. Lunch is eaten any time between 11.00am and 1.00pm, and is often a hot meal with plenty of liquids.

The afternoon's walk will normally end at around 4.00pm, giving the chance to write journal notes, read or chat with other members of the group while camp is being set up and the evening meal prepared. This is usually finished by 6.30 or 7.00pm allowing plenty of time to rest, read, talk or listen to the songs of the Sherpas beneath a starlit sky.

One of the many positive aspects of trekking with a group is that with trained cook and kitchen staff as part of the crew, the standard of food hygiene can be controlled - an important matter over which independent tea-house trekkers have little influence in the lodges. A skilled Nepali cook will often provide a surprising variety of meals using just basic portable equipment, and is rightly seen in the trek crew hierarchy as number two after the sirdar.

Most companies are well aware of the need to adopt conservation practices, particularly with regard to cooking by kerosene or gas and never by wood fire; in fact it is a requirement of entry to the Sagarmatha National Park that no timber is cut for firewood. It is also important to ensure that all waste materials are disposed of in a suitable manner, and not to the detriment of the environment. The trek leader should make himself responsible for ensuring that his party leaves nothing but footprints.

Adventure travel companies regularly advertise in the outdoor press, and a number of these organise promotional slide shows during the winter months. These provide an ideal opportunity for potential clients to meet and question trek leaders and assess what's on offer. A list of UK based companies who promote treks in the Everest region is given in Appendix D.

Independent Trekking:

For experienced travellers who either enjoy, or are not averse to making all arrangements - such as organising visas, booking flights and hotels in Kathmandu, queuing for permits, buying bus tickets to Jiri, route-finding on trek, choosing meals and lodges - independent tea-house trekking is the answer. It can be extremely rewarding, as well as being the cheapest form of trekking, but to be successful it is essential to adopt a flexible attitude of mind and be ready to adapt to a wide variety of circumstances. The only predictable element of travel in a country such as Nepal is the certainty that the unpredictable will happen!

Bufo Ventures (3 Elim Grove, Windermere) specialise in arranging treks for individuals and groups (but not backpackers), so if you want the freedom of independent trekking without the hassle of organisation, write for their details.

Tea-house trekking is understandably popular in Solu-Khumbu, not least because the quality of some of the lodges there is equalled only by the very best Thakali-run establishments in the Annapurna region. Lodges and/or tea-houses occur with great frequency most of the way from Jiri to Namche, while even above Namche it's possible to get accommodation right to the very foot of the biggest mountain of them all, thus enabling the trekker to travel with a minimum amount of equipment.

As far as this guidebook is concerned, a tea-house is a trailside building that offers basic refreshment for travellers; a lodge is a simple hotel (*bhatti*) where both food and shelter are provided. These *bhatti* are variously advertised as guest-houses, hotels, inns or lodges; but whatever the sign says outside, standards of accommodation are fairly basic - although inevitably some places provide a greater degree of comfort and a better standard of service than others. It should also be borne in mind that the provision of accommodation for trekkers is undergoing constant change and improvement.

In many villages 'Sherpa Guide Lodges' will be seen. These are part of a network whose standard of accommodation is generally higher than average. Contrary to the information given in another popular Nepal guidebook, it is not usually necessary to pre-book a bed in one of these, although as some trekking groups stay exclusively in such lodges, there may be occasions when all beds are taken.

Most *bhatti* consist of a simple building (sometimes an adaptation of a private home, sometimes purpose-built) comprising kitchen, dining area and sleeping quarters. The majority have dormitory accommodation, but a number also offer twin-bedded rooms. Washing facilities (where they exist) are fairly primitive, but most lodge owners will happily provide a small bowl of warm water to wash in. Some advertise hot showers; but if you imagine neat, tiled cubicles and abundant hot water, forget it. Often the 'shower' will consist of an outside shed with a hose of luke-warm water. Just occasionally you'll be pleasantly surprised, but don't bank on it, and as most showers are heated by dwindling stocks of firewood, you should seriously consider limiting the demand by showering only in those lodges using solar or kerosene-powered water heating. Toilets usually consist of a simple outbuilding with a hole in the floor over a pit. One memorable *charpi* at a Dingboche lodge had just three low walls and neither roof nor door. But it did have a magnificent view of the South Face of Lhotse - a true loo with a view! It is worth stressing, however, that standards are improving, and the majority of toilets should be quite acceptable. Just a few make you yearn for constipation. But whatever the general condition of lodge toilets, their use is preferable to treating the countryside as an open-air latrine.

Dormitories may accommodate as many as twenty trekkers, but they're usually more spacious than, say, those of mountain huts in the European Alps. Twin-bedded rooms are no more than a small bare 'cell' furnished with two firm but adequate beds. Each bed has a thin foam-rubber mattress and often a pillow. Blankets are not supplied. Trekkers are advised to use an insulation mat (Karrimat or similar) for additional comfort and as a barrier against possible infestation from some of the mattresses provided. There will be no floor covering. The walls consist of little more than thin wooden planks that offer no sound-proofing at all, and very rarely will there be even a hook from which to hang a few items of clothing or a towel. It's worth carrying a length of string and a couple of small screw-hooks to make your own portable clothes line. Bedrooms (other than dormitories) are usually made secure with a padlock.

Experienced trekkers quickly note the position of the kitchen fire and request a bed in a room well away from the possibility of escaping smoke. In some of the higher lodges a stove, or a pipe leading from a stove situated elsewhere, will help to heat the dormitory - with varying degrees of success.

A growing number of villages now boast electricity generated by small hydro schemes. Their lodges (and others with solar panels) will then have modest electric lighting. Even so, dining rooms are often poorly lit, but in the best of them a convivial atmosphere is easily created. Since the hill people of Nepal have little concept of privacy, none should be expected. The children of lodge owners will often join you at table, pick up your books or camera, study your clothes and anything else left lying around. If you find this curiosity annoying, don't provide temptation, set firm limits but don't lose your temper. This is their home, their country, and you are the guest who walked through an open door.

Bhatti offer a surprising choice of meals. First-time trekkers who arrive expecting to exist on a diet of *daal bhat* three times a day will be pleasantly surprised by the quality of lodge menus. On the trail to Everest it's possible to vary your diet between Western and local food, although it is important to remember that most lodge meals are cooked over a single fire, and if several trekkers order a variety of meals, it follows that some will inevitably have to wait a very long time before being served. Not only can this prove irksome (especially if you're hungry after a long day's trek), it also means that more firewood than necessary is being consumed. Assess what your fellow trekkers are ordering, and follow their lead. Most lodges have a few luxury items for sale: bottled drinks, biscuits, chocolate and sometimes tinned fruit.

Many lodge owners now display certificates announcing that they've completed a course in lodge management. This should lead to improved hygiene in food preparation, but a few common-sense precautions by trekkers will help minimise the risk of stomach upsets: always wash your hands before meals; make sure the crockery and cutlery provided is both clean and dry; and exercise caution in your choice of food and drinks.

The standard procedure on arrival at a lodge is to enquire of the owner if there are vacancies. If so, make your bed early. Find out what and where the washing and toilet facilities are, and if there is a set time by which to order meals. All food and drinks ordered should be entered in a notebook provided by the lodge keeper, and payment made prior to departure. Often you'll be trusted to add up the cost of each item ordered (listed on the house menu). Prices are exceedingly modest by Western standards, and the cost of accommodation so low that the lodge keeper relies on selling meals and drinks to make a reasonable living. Do not book a bed in one lodge and eat elsewhere, otherwise you'll be charged much more for your accommodation. Remember, too, that the farther you trek from the roadhead, the higher prices will be.

Independent trekkers are able to enjoy a much more flexible

routine than those on an organised trek, and can vary their route at will. Although there is a danger of mixing only with fellow Westerners, those who wish to learn more about local people, customs and the life of villages along the route will find that opportunities abound. However, the best way to enjoy cultural interaction is with the third method of trekking, in the company of a porter-guide.

Trekking with a Porter-Guide:

The best porter-guides become your trusty friends and companions who provide a daily insight into the ways of the people whose country you're travelling through. The opportunity for regular cultural exchange can be a highlight of any trek. A porter-guide will carry some of your gear, make sure you keep on the correct trail and act as a link between yourself and locals met on the path. If he's a Khumbu Sherpa, you will no doubt be invited into his home to meet other members of his family. He may suggest alternative trails and take you to sites of interest well off the normal route of most trekkers.

A good porter-guide can teach you much of value and, if you're sensitive, eager to learn and prepared to treat your companion as a friend rather than a servant, your experience will be the more profound as a result. Porter-guides may be hired in Kathmandu through one of the many trekking agencies based there (see Appendix D).

Of course, in such a well trekked and documented region as Solu-Khumbu, it's not essential to have a guide simply to keep you on the correct trail. However, on occasion you may feel the need to have someone carry your rucksack for you. In this case a porter is all that you need, and it's often possible to hire one along the route at short notice - either for just a day or two, or for the duration of the trek. Enquire of your lodge keeper for a reputable local - preferably one who speaks a few words of English. Payment is usually based on a set fee per day, inclusive of food and lodging, or a higher wage with the requirement that he provides his own food. It is worth remembering that the role of a porter is by no means a demeaning one, for it has long formed a major source of employment throughout the hill regions of Nepal.

Once you hire a man you assume employer's responsibility for his well-being. This includes making sure that he is adequately clothed and equipped to cope with below-freezing temperatures if your proposed route reaches high altitudes (as at Lobuche or Gorak Shep, for example). While a porter-guide hired from a Kathmandu agency may be expected to be well equipped, if you take on a porter from the lowlands he is not likely to have anything more than the clothes he stands up in, and it will be up to you to provide him with warm clothing once you get high. It is worth noting that duvets, boots and other gear can be rented in Namche Bazaar.

The easiest, most lightweight and inexpensive form of trekking with a porter-guide is to use lodges for overnight accommodation. Once you decide to camp you enter a more complicated style, with a leaning towards an organised trek. The more equipment needed, the more porters you'll require to carry it. In Kathmandu there are plenty of trekking agents who, within a few days of arrival, can supply all the manpower and equipment needed.

One final point: for safety purposes trekking alone is not recommended. If you'd rather not travel in an organised group and have no friend to trek with, it's possible to advertise for a companion in Kathmandu at the office of the Himalayan Rescue Association which is situated near the Central Immigration Office. The alternative is to hire a porter or porter-guide.

EVEREST TREKS

I felt I could go on like this for ever, that life had little better to offer than to march day after day in an unknown country to an unattainable goal. (H.W. Tilman)

Considering the amount of trekkers and mountaineers who have followed these trails, the route to Everest is no longer unknown country, even if, for the vast majority of those who go to seek its inspiration, Everest itself remains an unattainable goal. But the spirit of Tilman's statement is one which many trekkers will echo with feeling.

Everest being the focus, all trek routes automatically converge on the Sherpa capital of Namche Bazaar, which is situated about 45 kilometres (28 miles) to the south-west above the confluence of the Bhote Kosi and Dudh Kosi rivers. Above Namche further options become possible. Since the choice of route will depend largely on the amount of time available, an indication of the length of each trek is given below, but remember to add acclimatisation days once you reach Namche.

Jiri to Namche Bazaar: (6-9 days up; 4-5 days down)

This is the classic walk-in which follows the trail used by the first successful expedition to climb Mount Everest in 1953, and which has been adopted by just about every subsequent mountaineering expedition destined for the Khumbu. Rich in contrasts, it provides the best possible introduction to the area. There are plenty of tea-houses and lodges along the way, thus making it an ideal route for independent trekkers as well as those in organised groups choosing to camp overnight. As the trail has been regularly used by Westerners for many years, it is not surprising to find that some of the lodges here are among the best in all Nepal.

Jiri lies in the foothills just west of the valley of the Khimti Khola, and may be reached from Kathmandu following a long day's journey by public bus. Leaving Jiri the trek heads roughly eastwards across the grain of the land, and by way of a series of high ridges meets the major valley of the Dudh Kosi after 3 or 4 days. (There is an alternative start which avoids the long road journey to Jiri and instead makes use of the STOL airstrip at Phaplu in the valley of the Solu Khola below Junbesi. This option makes it possible to reach Namche in about 4-5 days; allow 3-4 days back.)

As far as the Dudh Kosi this first part of the trek is quite strenuous with much height gain and loss. Vegetation is lush and varied with the hillsides either forested, or terraced for agriculture. Views of distant mountains tease day after day. The highest point reached is the pass of Lamjura La at 3530m (11,581ft), which is even higher than Namche Bazaar, but after crossing the Dudh Kosi below Manidingma (also known as Nuntala), the route heads north to rise steadily over successive mountain spurs, passing below Lukla and reaching Namche with big snowpeaks rising all around.

Lukla to Namche Bazaar: (1½ days up; 1 day down)

Flying in to Lukla is the choice of those with only a limited amount of time to devote to a trek. During the main trekking seasons flights

24

from Kathmandu are scheduled daily, but these rely on clear, settled conditions. Low-lying clouds at any time of year can and do cause delays. Once safely landed at Lukla (2850m: 9350ft) it is important not to rush upvalley ignoring the need to acclimatise, but make an easy 1¹/₂-day hike to Namche, joining the main trail from Jiri at Chaunrikharka.

Namche Bazaar to Lobuche and Gorak Shep: (4-5 days up; 2 days down)

The nearest lodge accommodation to the base of Mount Everest is at Gorak Shep on the west bank of the Khumbu glacier, just beyond the point where it is joined by the Khangri Shar and Khangri Nup glaciers. Everest Base Camp is about 2 hours further upvalley, while directly above Gorak Shep rises the great viewpoint of Kala Pattar. About 6 kilometres (4 miles) down-valley, set in a wide ablation trough, are the lodges of Lobuche where most independent trekkers prefer to stay. Both Lobuche and Gorak Shep have camping areas.

The trail to Everest Base Camp and Kala Pattar is well trodden and visually spectacular. Because of the altitude it is important to advance in easy stages, and it is recommended that at least two nights be spent in Namche (or at one or other of its neighbouring villages) before moving on, and take another acclimatisation rest at Pheriche or Dingboche.

Above Namche the valley forks. The left branch leads to Gokyo and the headwaters of the Dudh Kosi; the right-hand option entices with the summit of Everest seen peering over the huge wall that appears to block the valley of the Imja Khola. Thyangboche is a wooded ridge near the junction of these two valleys, a day's walk from Namche. Leaving Thyangboche the trail goes to Pangboche, beyond which there are no more villages until after the next fork in the valley.

Here the right branch is the Imja valley, with lodges at Dingboche and Chhukhung. The main trail takes the left-hand option below Dingboche and leads to Pheriche, Lobuche and Gorak Shep. An alternative trail links Dingboche with Pheriche, and yet another cuts round the slopes of Pokalde to join the main trail near the simple lodges of Dughla about 1¹/₂-2 hours below Lobuche. At least two nights should be spent at either Lobuche or Gorak Shep in order to have time to visit Kala Pattar or Everest Base Camp.

Namche Bazaar to Gokyo: (3-4 days up; 1½ days down)

Although Gokyo is not very far from Namche in linear distance, the advanced altitude demands short stages to get there. There are two alternatives for the first stage; one goes via Khumjung, the other takes the main Thyangboche trail as far as Kyangjuma before climbing the hillside to join the path from Khumjung.

The Gokyo trail keeps on the west side of the Dudh Kosi valley, crosses one or two tributary glens and passes a few simple lodges before reaching the snout of Nepal's largest glacier, the Ngozumpa. Several charming lakes lie in the ablation valley below the glacier's moraine wall, and the lodges of Gokyo overlook the third of these, with Gokyo Ri rising above its northern shore. A climb to this tremendous viewpoint is highly recommended, while other places of interest upvalley would repay several days based at Gokyo.

In good conditions experienced trekkers could cross the Cho La (5420m: 17,782ft) to reach Dughla or Lobuche in a long, hard day. An alternative is to descend back through the Dudh Kosi valley via its eastern side to Phortse, and next day continue to Thyangboche or Namche.

Other trek suggestions for the Everest region, on the Tibetan side as well as in Nepal, appear elsewhere in this book.

TREKKING SEASONS

No-one ever travelled far during the monsoon if he could help it.
(Eric Shipton)

Whilst trekking may be possible at any time of year in Solu-Khumbu there are generally considered to be two main seasons: the spring, pre-monsoon period, and the post-monsoon months before winter sets in.

The post-monsoon period, which begins in late-September and continues until the arrival of winter in December, is the most popular. Trails and lodges will then be at their busiest, the weather is generally settled, but when rain does fall it is usually short-lived. Days are blessed with clear, often cloud-free skies with a magical light ideal for photography. Day-time temperatures are very pleasant. Above Namche nights can be chilly in October, while at Gokyo, Thyangboche and beyond heavy frosts should be expected. By mid-November night-time temperatures will have dropped to well below freezing, although views by day have a lustre unrivalled at any other time of the year.

In mid-winter (December-January) the intense cold experienced above Namche Bazaar can make nights especially uncomfortable, and in some years heavy snowfall in the higher regions can make travel difficult or even impossible. In addition some of the lodges may be closed, thus putting a few areas effectively out of bounds to independent trekkers. Late-winter (February-March) is sometimes disrupted by snowstorms. Not only can these cause severe trail problems, but on occasion flights are unable to land at Lukla for several days at a time. In Khumbu March has a reputation for being as cold as, or colder than, December, but the walk-in from Jiri can be extremely pleasant with plenty of bird activity and rhododendrons splashing the hillsides with extravagant colour.

The spring trekking season runs from late-March to May. In the lower hills temperatures rise considerably, and by May the first few days of a trek from Jiri may be extremely warm - especially for independent travellers carrying large rucksacks. Haze can also spoil distant views, although at higher elevations the atmosphere is generally clear and temperatures moderate. This is the season for the keen botanist, for numerous varieties of wild flowers will be found in bloom throughout the region.

From June to September Nepal is affected by the monsoon. During this time paths can be treacherous with mud, rivers and streams become raging torrents, torrential rain and mist deny views for much of the day, and trees, shrubs and undergrowth are infested with leeches. However, the countryside is then green and lush, wild flowers are impressive, and when clouds shred and momentarily part the mountains reveal an undeniable drama. There are very few trekkers along the trails, and village life resumes its age-old pattern. Anyone tempted to trek during the monsoon, though, should be aware that paths may be re-routed, some bridges could be washed away and lengthy diversions become necessary.

ENVIRONMENTAL CONSIDERATIONS AND CULTURAL INTERACTION

Everything is good when it leaves the Creator's hands; everything degenerates in the hands of man. (Jean-Jacques Rousseau)

Since the first officially sanctioned trek to the Everest region took place in 1964, and following the construction of the airstrip at Lukla the following year, there has been a massive increase in the number of visitors to Khumbu - not only trekkers, but anthropologists, aid workers and mountaineers whose forerunners first opened the eyes of the developed world to the scenic and cultural riches of the area. The resulting people-pressure has imposed great demands on the environment and has had a profound effect upon the economy and lifestyle of local people.

If today's trekkers are to limit their impact on the area, and on those who live there, it is necessary to take stock of the problems that exist, and to learn from past mistakes.

Much has been written about deforestation caused by an expanding population and the requirements of large numbers of trekkers. Much publicity (some quite justified, but some ill-informed) has been given to problems of litter and the disposal of human waste; others complain about inappropriate or badly planned forms of development.

Yet the passage of time has not been entirely negative, for the natural beauty of the mountains, as seen from the trekking trails, remains untainted. As for the Sherpas, in the main they are every bit as hospitable, warm-hearted and friendly as their reputation suggests. They are not, of course, simple mountain peasants, for education is widely available (thanks to Sir Edmund Hillary's Himalayan Trust), and the comparative wealth brought by mountaineering expeditions and thousands of trekkers has helped improve the lot of a number of lodge and tea-house owners, some of whom may have travelled as widely as the trekkers who use their facilities.

The establishment of the Sagarmatha National Park, and its elevation to World Heritage Site status, has helped focus attention on some of the environmental problems and begun seriously to address them. Small hydro schemes have been set up in selected areas (in Khumbu and in the middle hills), bringing partial relief from demands for firewood, and the Himalayan Trust is tackling the question of deforestation through the development of local tree nurseries. The Park authorities have put a ban on cutting trees, but firewood and construction timber is regularly brought in from outside the Park, so a local problem has merely been transferred elsewhere.

Litter is a world-wide problem, not one that is confined to the popular trails and campsites of Nepal. Yet what we refuse to see in our own society becomes an eyesore in those places we visit on holiday. Litter found on the trails leading to Everest - from toilet paper to cigarette butts and sweet wrappers - however, can almost entirely be blamed on Western visitors. In the words of Oscar Wilde, 'Each man kills the thing he loves'.

Happily the 'Kleenex Trail' is not as bad as some adverse publicity might suggest, and several well publicised clean-up expeditions have improved the base camp of Mount Everest itself, while many trekkers' campsites, despite heavy usage, are much tidier than has sometimes been the case. Dozens of rubbish disposal pits have been dug by the Sherpas, and community incinerators provided in some villages.

But there is no room for complacency, and every traveller lured by the Shangri La promise of Solu-Khumbu has a responsibility to respect the values and virtues of this magical land, to do nothing to detract from it, but rather to treat the landscape and those who live in it with sensitivity, respect and love.

A need for environmental awareness on trek cannot be over-stated. To this end the Kathmandu Environmental Education Project (KEEP) has set up an information centre on Tridevi Marg, Kathmandu, near the Central Immigration Office. Do find time to visit this before heading for the hills.

When it comes to cross-cultural interaction, most of us are innocents abroad. Our Western society is no preparation for the kaleidoscopic cultures of the East, yet it is sheer arrogance to assume that our ways are superior to those of the Nepali hill folk. Their culture has developed separately from ours, and observation of its intricacies is an important ingredient in successful trekking. If we wish to gain maximum benefit from the trekking experience, we must observe all we can. Then we may discover our hosts have more to teach us with regard to living in contentment than we can possibly teach them. In the unfussed ways of simple villagers we learn that patience, kindness and tolerance for all are virtues worth striving for. In turn it is necessary for us to observe certain rules of behaviour in order to avoid giving offence to our hosts. The following guidelines, once studied, should become second nature after a few days on the trail.

Affection: Avoid public displays of affection. Kissing, cuddling and even holding hands in public are frowned upon by local people.

Begging: In general don't encourage it. Children who ask for school pens, balloons, money or candy should be discouraged. Helping children become beggars will only erode their self-respect.

Campfires: Conserve wood. Resist the temptation to have a campfire, and only trek with groups that guarantee to cook on kerosene or gas stoves. When using lodges, limit your demand for hot showers to those places where water is heated by solar or hydro power.

Dress: A state of undress is unacceptable in both sexes. Men should not bare their chests in public, nor should women wear revealing blouses. Tight-fitting clothes should be avoided; women ought to wear either a long loose skirt or slacks, not shorts.

Food: Do not touch food or utensils that Nepalis will use. Never give or take food with the left hand. If cutlery is unavailable, use only your right hand for eating.

Haggling: Whilst haggling is part of the trade culture of Kathmandu, never haggle over prices in tea-houses or lodges on trek. Do not condone over-charging, but pay the going rate. Prices are often set by the local community.

The hearth: Never discard rubbish onto your host's fire, no matter how small and insignificant it may seem. Nor should you sit next to it in a Nepali home unless specifically invited to do so.

Legs & feet: The soles of your feet should not be pointed at a Nepali, nor should legs be so outstretched that they need to be stepped over. Nepalis will not step over legs or feet.

Litter: Do not leave litter - anywhere. Carry strong waterproof bags to take out non-burnable, non-degradable rubbish. Remove all unnecessary wrappings before leaving home. Ensure campsites are left free from rubbish, and encourage sirdars, trek crew and porters to follow conservation measures.

Monasteries: When visiting monasteries remove your boots or shoes before entering, and make a donation.

Photography: Be discreet when taking photographs of local people. Remember, you are not in a zoo, nor a museum. Establish a relationship with your subject where possible, and ask permission before taking someone's photograph. Respect their right to say no.

Prayer walls: Always pass to the left of prayer walls (mani walls), chortens and stupas.

Short-cuts: Stick to trails and avoid trampling plants. Taking short-cuts can add to problems of soil erosion.

Smile: Act with patience and friendliness towards local people - and smile. Nepalis smile a lot. That warmth should be reflected back.

Toilets: No matter how primitive or unsanitary some lodge toilets may seem, do make use of the facilities provided. If it is completely unavoidable and you must defecate where no toilet is available, always bury your faeces well away from water sources, and burn used toilet paper. On group treks ensure that toilet tents are set up at least 50 metres from any water source, and dig holes at least 50 centimetres (18 inches) deep.

Touching: Never touch a Nepali on the head, and do not touch anyone with your shoes.

Water: Do not bathe or wash clothes in streams. Use natural or biodegradable soaps and dispose of used water well away from streams.

Wealth: Be discreet when handling money; do not tempt locals into envy by making an obvious display of the contents of your wallet. Keep a few small denomination rupee notes handy for paying bills along the way. Don't leave valuable items unattended.

Finally, the word *Namaste*, given with palms pressed together as if in prayer, is the universal greeting of Nepal; it means 'I salute the God within you' and will be well received when offered to a Nepali on trail, in villages or in lodges and tea-houses. Use it with a smile - and mean it. From such simple beginnings may grow a flower of understanding.

PRE-DEPARTURE PREPARATIONS

The journey should be carefully planned beforehand, especial study being given to the matter of gradients. (Karl Baedeker)

This guidebook has not been produced to encourage more trekkers to explore the trails of Solu-Khumbu, but hopefully to add something to the experience of those already committed to going there. Since it is better to be forewarned than to walk blindly into disappointment, this particular section should strip away the veneer of romance and expose the bare reality for those considering their first trek.

The highest mountains in the world attract numerous trekkers to their valleys, many of whom have neither undertaken a multi-day walk before, nor had any previous mountain experience. Mount Everest becomes a collector's item for world travellers, alongside the Pyramids of Egypt and the Taj Mahal. That so many survive the experience to return for more says as much for the spell cast by the fabled Himalaya as for the care and attention devoted to them by their trek organisers and crew.

Successful trekking may be described as the art of gaining most from the multitude of experiences on offer. But to achieve that requires as much mental preparation as physical fitness. Tackling a journey on foot that will demand 2 or 3 weeks of effort is a far different proposition to that of a fortnight's holiday based in one village from which to set out on day walks whenever the mood arises. As a member of an organised group trek you will be expected to walk day after day, rain or shine, whether you feel up to it or not. Naturally, real infirmity is excluded, but trail weariness is not. So get yourself both mentally and physically fit before boarding the plane to Kathmandu.

Consider the following scenario: of waking one morning weary from past excesses and feeling queasy from a stomach upset. Consider a cold wind and falling rain and a trek leader cajoling you to start walking. You have about 8 hours of uphill trail ahead of you before the next camp is set up - and there's no alternative but to pull on your

---

The all-seeing eyes of the Buddha overlook the Kathmandu valley from Swayambhunath

Between Junbesi and Salung the trail turns a corner to find a long row of snowpeaks on the horizon. Everest is just seen at far left

The scene at Lukla

boots and waterproofs and start moving.

In certain seasons and in parts of the Khumbu region there may well be extended periods of intense cold to put up with, of days without being able to have a decent wash, or several nights in a row when you've not been able to enjoy restful sleep. Perhaps you're slow to adapt to the altitude; maybe the diet is not to your liking or, if you're new to camping, you've discovered you don't like sleeping in a tent. (It happens, so do try a night or two camping out before you commit yourself to a trek that uses tents.) On a tea-house trek you could be dismayed by the standard of accommodation provided, or by the lack of hygiene. There will be times of confusion, times when your Western sensibilities are appalled by the different values accepted by those whose country you are wandering through.

Successful trekking demands an ability to adapt to a whole range of ever-changing circumstances, to put Western values on hold and be prepared to accept that there could be much to learn about living from Nepali hill culture. Learning to respect unfamiliar ways is in itself sometimes a shock to the system.

But if you're convinced that wandering among the most dramatic scenery on earth, of mingling daily with people of an entirely foreign culture, and that a sense of achievement at the end of the trek offer sufficient rewards for the odd day of misery and discomfort - then trekking is for you. If you have doubts, forget it. Five or six days into a long walk is not the time to decide that trekking is too alien an exercise for enjoyment. The financial outlay required to undertake a trek in Nepal should be sufficient spur to ensure that you enjoy every moment of your time there. Don't waste it on doubts or inadequate preparation.

As a member of an organised trek you have a duty to your fellow group members and to the leader to arrive in good shape, with fitness to match your enthusiasm. Trails are uncompromisingly steep in places, and there's only one real way to get physically fit for trekking in the Himalaya, and that is by walking up and down hills. Jogging will help build stamina and endurance, swimming and cycling are also beneficial, but uphill walking with a rucksack is the best possible preparation. If hills are in short supply near your home, just walk as far and as often as you can wherever is convenient. Once you arrive in Nepal and the trail winds ahead as far as the eye can see, you'll be glad you put in some effort at home.

Having decided to go trekking towards Everest, put most of your preconceived ideas behind you, open your eyes, your mind and your heart to all that Nepal has to offer, and set forth with a determination to see and to understand. You'll soon discover that the mountains are only part of the charm. As has been pointed out by a number of experienced trekkers, few will be content with just one Himalayan journey. 'The trek of a lifetime' is likely to be the first of many.

EQUIPMENT CHECK-LIST

Having only brought one coat, which was wet, spent the evening in a sweater. Luckily I had two. (G.H. Bullock, writing from 20,000ft on Mount Everest)

Bullock took part in the first Everest reconnaissance expedition of 1921, when clothing and equipment used by the climbers was unbelievably basic - he even carried some of his gear in an old suitcase! When we compare that with some of the state-of-the-art gear worn by a few once-only trekkers on the Khumbu trail today we can see just how far equipment design and manufacture has advanced. This is not the place to discuss the merits of one product against another, but to provide a list of items likely to be needed by trekkers using this book.

Rucksack (day-sack only for members of an organised group trek)
Kitbag (group trekkers only; these fit onto a porter's doko)
Boots (lightweight are best; also spare laces & cleaning kit)
Light shoes (trainers preferred)
Socks (outer & inner)
Trousers/breeches (light cotton for travel, hotel use & on trek; plus thicker pair for cold conditions)
Long, loose skirt for women
Shirts (1 for travel, 2 or 3 for trek)

Underwear (include thermal wear for cold conditions)
Sleeping bag (4 seasons plus; also sleeping bag liner)
Insulation mat (Karrimat or similar)
Gloves (thermal inner & warm outer mitts)
Balaclava (or woollen hat)
Sunhat & sunglasses
Water bottle (1 litre capacity)
Headtorch, spare bulb & batteries
Mending kit

Sweater (or fibre-pile jacket)
Down jacket
Cagoule & overtrousers
Whistle
Plastic bags
Penknife
Small padlock (to secure kitbag for group trekkers, or to lock bedroom if staying in lodges)
Water filter (optional for independent trekkers)

Toilet kit (incl. 2 small towels)
Toilet paper (& lighter)
First aid kit
Map & compass
Guidebook
Notebook & pens
Camera & films (also spare batteries & lens tissues)
Passport (& passport photos)
Trekking pole/walking stick

It is good to have a complete change of clothes waiting for your return from trek, and most Kathmandu hotels have a storage facility. Make sure your left luggage is secure and clearly marked with your name and expected date of return.

A trekking pole has been added to the above list as experience proves their value in aiding balance on stream-crossings, on trails slippery with a morning glaze of ice, and on steep descents where they are especially useful for anyone with problem knees. A trekking pole is really a ski stick in all but name. Used for decades by mountain walkers on the Continent, they are gaining in popularity among British trekkers too. The best of these poles are lightweight but strong, and are telescopic so that the length can easily and quickly be changed to suit. When reduced to minimum length they will often fit inside a kitbag or backpack for ease of transportation on airlines.

There is a tendency by some group trekkers to take far too much clothing and equipment with them, knowing that porters or yaks will shoulder the burden. As Baedeker once wrote, 'To be provided with enough and no more may be considered the second golden rule of the traveller'. Don't be tempted to pack too much. Remember that most airlines have a free baggage allowance of only 20kgs (44lbs), and there's no need to go to the limit.

PERMITS AND VISAS

*And the end of the fight is a tombstone white with the name
of the late deceased/And the epitaph drear: A fool lies here
who tried to hustle the East.* (Rudyard Kipling)

All foreigners, except Indian nationals, require a valid passport and
tourist visa to enter Nepal. Visa applications should be made direct
to the Nepalese Embassy or Consulate in your home country
(addresses are given in Appendix C), a straightforward process that
involves minimal form-filling, the provision of two passport
photographs and payment of the appropriate fee (check current
prices with the Embassy). Postal applications should be made at least
one month before the date of departure. Don't forget to include a
stamped addressed envelope for the return of your passport. Postal
applications ought to be made by registered post or recorded delivery,
and the envelope clearly marked 'Visa application'. If you apply in
person at the Embassy, be warned that you will not be able to collect
it until next day. Visas are valid for a period of 3 months after the date
of issue, and have a duration of 30 days.

A 30-day visa is at present possible to arrange upon arrival at
Tribhuvan International Airport, Kathmandu. Unless there's a large
queue, formalities are dealt with very quickly. Application forms are
available at the airport, but make sure you have passport photographs
and the correct fee in US dollars.

Should you plan to be in Nepal for longer than 30 days you'll need
a visa extension. Up to two extensions of a month each may be
obtained for most tourist visas, but after 3 months you will be
expected to leave the country for at least a month before being
allowed to return. It is only permissible to be in Nepal for a maximum
of 4 months in any 12-month period. If you're with an organised trek,
your trekking company will arrange extensions on your behalf. But
for independent travellers visa extensions must be purchased in
Kathmandu at the Central Immigration Office on Tridevi Marg,
between Kantipath and Thamel (or, if you plan to visit the Annapurna
region after Everest, at the Immigration Office near Damside in
Pokhara). Applications must be accompanied by passport, passport

photographs and appropriate fee. On occasion independent travellers need to show proof of the amount of foreign currency exchanged within the country - sometimes it is necessary to change a set sum for every day on trek. This requirement changes from time to time with little advance warning, so be prepared by keeping bank exchange receipts, and make a photocopy of each one in case proof is demanded. Instant passport photo facilities, and photocopying machines, are situated near the Immigration Office in Kathmandu.

A trekking permit is required for travel outside the Kathmandu valley and Pokhara, the fee for which is based upon the number of days of its validity - so much for each week of the trek's duration. If your trek is of 9 days duration, you will need a 2-week permit. The approved route is outlined on each permit by naming the main villages and districts to be visited. They must be submitted for inspection at police check-posts along the trail. Note that if you plan to trek in more than one region, a permit will be required for each trek. Entry to the Sagarmatha National Park also requires a permit. Both this and the trekking permit are issued at the Central Immigration Office.

Application forms are available at the entrance to the office where a list of current rules and regulations is posted. In addition to your passport and valid visa, you will need two passport photos and, possibly, photocopies of bank exchange receipts - depending on regulations in force at the time. Applications can usually be dealt with the same day (check what time you must return to collect the permit), but at the height of the trekking season it may be necessary to wait up to 3 days before permits are ready.

Offices are open Sunday to Thursday 10.00am to 2.00pm, and Friday morning from 10.00 till noon. Beware of the many official holidays and festivals that occur with some frequency and can leave you kicking your heels for days whilst waiting for the office to re-open. In the main trekking season queues are exceedingly long and progress seems painfully slow. However, the clerks dealing with an avalanche of applications work under considerable pressure and need your understanding, not expressions of frustration. (When tempted to curse the bureaucratic form filling and long hours spent standing in queues, consider the treatment handed out to certain foreign nationals by some immigration officials at major airports in the UK and other Western capitals.)

If you cannot face the queues, or are short of time in Kathmandu to arrange everything, consider using an agent to obtain permits and visa extensions on your behalf. There are many agents with offices in Thamel and on Durbar Marg who will happily deal with the bureaucracy - for a fee. It will not be cheap, but you may well feel it is money worth spending. Do not be tempted to buy either trekking permits or visa extensions on the black market. Westerners have languished in Nepalese gaols with plenty of time to regret having done so. The fee you pay for the privilege of trekking in Nepal is, after all, an important source of revenue for one of the poorest countries in the world.

HEALTH MATTERS

Those with weak hearts, palpitations, and so forth must, of course, avoid ascents altogether. (Karl Baedeker)

For a normal active person in good physical condition, trekking in Nepal should not present any undue health risk. Yet first-time visitors to the Himalaya often become obsessed by their health, and there are occasions when the trails of Nepal become hypochondriacs' highways. Conversations in tea-houses and lodges alike zone in on topics related to bowel and bladder movement, on concerns related to the digestive tract, headaches, chest infections and the fear of altitude sickness. Obviously the farther you wander from 'civilisation' the more important it is to look after your health, but don't allow these concerns to become obsessive.

Prior to leaving home it would be wise for anyone with a particular worry to undergo a thorough medical examination, and it is important to have those inoculations deemed necessary by the health authorities before you go. Take a first aid kit with you, adopt a sensible attitude towards food and hygiene - and trust to luck. Overall, trekking is a healthy pursuit. Things will not be as they are at home, but if you expect there to be no risk at all when wandering in a developing country, save your money or book a holiday elsewhere.

Immunisation:

Nepal does not require visitors to show proof of immunisation, unless travelling by way of an infected area, but vaccination against the following is recommended: tuberculosis (BCG), typhoid, tetanus, meningitis and hepatitis. Should your journey to Nepal pass through a region where yellow fever is prevalent, you must be vaccinated against this also. You may need to show a valid certificate of inoculation for this on entry.

Rabies exists in Nepal and there is a slight chance (estimated at 1 in 6000) that you might be bitten whilst in the country. Bearing in mind that the disease is fatal, you may wish to consider vaccination against it. It is rather expensive, however. As a precaution, do not approach or fuss dogs or monkeys.

As certain vaccinations need to be taken some time before travelling, visit your doctor 2 or 3 months before the date your trek is due to commence.

Malaria:

If you plan to visit the Terai during your time in Nepal, or travel by way of Bangladesh or India, you may be advised to embark on a course of anti-malaria tablets. Check the requirement at least 2 weeks before going (see below).

Health Advice:

In addition to advice provided by your medical practitioner, up-to-date specialist health advice can be obtained in Britain from MASTA (Medical Advisory Services for Travellers Abroad) who for a fee will send printed information in response to a telephone request. The number to call is: 0171 631 4408 (between 9.30am and 5.00pm Monday to Friday). Their address is: MASTA, Keppel Street, London WC1E 7HT. MASTA also operate a Travellers' Health Line (01891 224100) which provides a health brief containing up-to-date information with regard to immunisations, malaria etc., and is tailored to specific journeys.

Anyone with a record of lung or heart disease should avoid treks that go to high altitudes, and should consult their doctor before committing themselves to a trip to Nepal. It is in any case sensible to have a medical check before setting off on a lengthy Himalayan trek.

Chest Problems:

Coughs, colds and chest infections are exacerbated by smoky lodges, dust and the dry cold air of high altitude. The sound of locals emptying their lungs with a serenade of coughing and spitting is the hill music of Nepal, to which most trekkers add voice at some time or other. Soluble lozenges will soothe inflamed throats, catarrh pastilles are worth taking, as are antibiotics (Ampicillin or as recommended) to combat chest infections.

Water:

The most frequent cause of health problems is via contaminated water. With poor sanitation, a variety of organisms live in the streams and rivers of Nepal, and all water in the country (including that supplied in hotels and restaurants in Kathmandu) should be considered suspect unless it has been vigorously boiled for 10 minutes, treated with iodine or comes in a bottle with an unbroken seal. Certain advanced water filtration systems, such as the portable Katadyn filter, claim to be effective even in removing *giardia* cysts, and could be worth using in the hills.

Iodine (Lugol's solution - available in Kathmandu pharmacies) is most often used by trekkers to treat suspect water, and should be carried in a small plastic dropper bottle protected against spillage. Eight drops per litre is the recommended amount. Leave for 20-30 minutes before drinking (longer for very cold or cloudy water). Many iodine bottles sold in Kathmandu have suspect screw tops, and you are advised to transfer the contents to a more leak-proof container.

On a group trek in the care of a reputable adventure travel company, the cook and kitchen crew will make every effort to ensure that all water is properly treated, and you should have no concerns on this score. However, if you are relying on food and drink from tea-houses and lodges, you should be a little more circumspect. Beware milk drinks and consume only those liquids you can be sure have been adequately boiled - such as tea. Nepalese bottled beer, Coca Cola and Fanta should give no cause for concern, and are widely available on the trail to Everest.

Remember that it is not only by drinking contaminated water that it's possible to contract something nasty, but also by using it when cleaning your teeth. If you cannot be certain about the quality of available water, do not even rinse your teeth with it.

Giardia:

Giardia lamblia is a tiny protozoan parasite whose cyst is prevalent in the streams of upland Nepal, and in many other parts of the world too (ie. it is not limited to developing countries). The parasite invades the upper part of the small intestine, can damage the gut lining, and is fairly common among trekkers. It can take 2 or 3 weeks after infection for symptoms to become apparent, and may result in sudden acute illness, or have a more long-lasting effect. One sure way of identifying a sufferer from *giardia* is by the foul-smelling, rotten-egg gases emitted. Although not life-threatening, *giardia* is still a major health risk - and it strains friendships. Symptoms include nausea, feeling bloated, stomach cramps after eating, weight loss and dehydration. Irregular bouts of diarrhoea accompanied by pale, greasy mucus also form part of the symptoms, but treatment is straightforward and fairly rapid. A course of tinidazole antibiotic (Tiniba is the brand name available in Kathmandu pharmacies) normally results in a complete cure. Dosage is 2gr in a single dose per day for 3 days.

Food and Hygiene:

Food is another problem area for independent trekkers, but with a little luck and forethought you should remain mostly trouble-free. Try to avoid uncooked fruit (unless you can peel it yourself), salad vegetables that may have been rinsed in untreated water, and certain foods that have been cooked and later reheated - lasagne is a prime example.

Most trekkers suffer a mild dose of diarrhoea (*Kathmandu Quickstep*) at some time or other during their stay in Nepal, although often this is simply reaction to a change of diet. Sufferers need not become unduly alarmed unless blood is passed in the stools (a sign of possible dysentery), for this usually remedies itself in a few days. Simply take plenty of liquids to prevent dehydration, reduce solid food intake and avoid dairy products and alcohol. A rehydration solution, such as Dioralyte or Jeevan Jal (the Nepalese brand obtained in Kathmandu) is quickly absorbed into the system and will help speed recovery.

Basic rules of hygiene, such as washing hands before meals and after going to the toilet, are obvious but should not be overlooked.

All food and drinks consumed in Kathmandu should be treated with the same circumspection as on trek. The time to relax your guard is when you arrive home. That being said, do keep your concerns in perspective and don't allow them to dominate your time in Nepal. With a little forethought and detail to personal hygiene, you should remain perfectly fit and healthy.

Mountain Sickness:
The other major concern of trekkers is that of altitude, or mountain, sickness. Acute Mountain Sickness (AMS) can affect anyone above an altitude of about 2000m (6500ft), but it is not possible to predict in advance who will suffer from it. Physical fitness is of no apparent benefit, nor is youthfulness. In fact it would appear that young people may be more susceptible to AMS than older trekkers.

AMS occurs as a result of the body failing to acclimatise adequately to reduced oxygen levels experienced at altitude. Nowhere along the trails of Solu-Khumbu is too high for a normal healthy body to acclimatise, given time, but some take much longer than others to adapt. By failing to allow sufficient time for acclimatisation, AMS is almost guaranteed to develop. The best way to avoid it is to ascend gradually once you reach 2000m (6500ft), and above 3000m (10,000ft) ascend no more than about 400m (1300ft) per day. On some sections of the trail it is not easy to follow the golden rule of 'climb high, sleep low' so it is important to make gradual height gain, with rest days, in order to allow the body to acclimatise properly.

Another important consideration is liquid intake. At altitude it is necessary to drink at least 4 litres (7 pints) a day in order to avoid dehydration, and to urinate a minimum of half a litre per day - a great deal of fluid is lost at altitude through breathing. Yellow-coloured urine is a sign that liquid intake needs to be increased.

With the onset of AMS fluid accumulates in the lungs or the brain or, in severe cases, in both. Recognition of the symptoms, and attention to reducing them, are both vital if serious illness or, at worst, death is to be avoided. Early symptoms of mild AMS to watch for are extreme fatigue, headache and loss of appetite. Some trekkers also find themselves breathless with only minimal exercise, and suffer disturbed sleep. When these symptoms develop do not go any higher until they have gone away. If they show no sign of leaving after a day or two, but instead become worse, it is important to descend to lower levels. Do not take sleeping tablets or strong pain killers at altitude, since these can mask some of the symptoms.

A worsening condition is indicated by vomiting, severe headache, lack of co-ordination, wet, bubbly breathing, increased tiredness and breathlessness even at rest. Such symptoms warn of the onset of a very serious condition which, if ignored, can lead to loss of consciousness and death within 12 hours. The only cure is to descend at once until symptoms decrease and finally disappear completely. An improvement will normally be felt after 300m (1000ft) or so of descent.

High Altitude Cerebral Oedema (HACE) and High Altitude Pulmonary Oedema (HAPE) occur as advanced stages of AMS and are both potential killers. Every year a number of trekkers die in Nepal through failure to recognise and respond to the symptoms. The only cure is either immediate descent to lower altitudes or, if one is available, to insert the patient into a Gamow Bag in which pressure is raised by means of a foot pump to simulate a lower altitude. (A Gamow Bag, or hyperbaric chamber, is kept at the Trekker's Aid Post in Pheriche.) In the case of HACE or HAPE no sufferer should be left to descend alone, nor should there be any delay. If symptoms occur at night do not wait until morning to descend.

As with all health concerns it is important to be aware of potential dangers, but keep them in perspective and do not allow your concern to devalue the pleasures of the trek. Be aware of symptoms, act upon them if they occur and, time and energy willing, continue with your trek when signs of improvement indicate.

Hospitals, Health Posts and Emergency Evacuation:

A Trekker's Aid Post established by the Himalayan Rescue Association (HRA) in 1973 is situated in Pheriche. During the main trekking seasons it is manned by volunteer doctors who specialise in altitude-related problems and attempt to educate trekkers to the dangers of going too high too fast. They give lectures each afternoon on the subject of mountain sickness, which are well worth attending, and are usually available for medical consultations. Consultations and treatment must be paid for, and those who attend lectures should make a donation towards the cost of running the Post.

It is also worth making a visit to the HRA office in Kathmandu (situated near the Central Immigration Office) prior to going on trek. Not only will you receive good advice on AMS and other health matters, but forms are available to enable you to register with your Embassy - very useful in the case of emergency.

There are small hospitals or health posts at Jiri, Phaplu, Junbesi and Khunde, in addition to the HRA post at Pheriche mentioned above. Namche Bazaar has a dental clinic. For emergency evacuation there are STOL airstrips at Jiri, Phaplu, Lukla and Syangboche, but flights are dependent on good weather conditions and should not be relied upon. Evacuation from the more remote areas of Khumbu is difficult to organise and extremely expensive to carry out. Rescues will only be attempted when a guarantee of payment has been made. It has been said that if you're trekking with a reputable adventure travel company and something goes wrong it may be possible to arrange emergency evacuation by air. If you're travelling independently, there's no chance at all.

Should you need to consult a Western doctor on return to Kathmandu, the best known clinic is that of the Canadian CIWEC situated opposite the Russian Embassy in Baluwatar (Tel: 410983). It is expensive, but facilities are said to be very good.

First Aid Kit:

All trekkers, whether travelling independently or with an organised group, should carry a personal first aid kit, the very minimum contents of which should be:

Sticky plaster dressing strips	Moleskin (for blisters)
Bandages (cotton gauze & elastic)	Paracetamol (or aspirin)
Throat lozenges (& cough pastilles)	Thermometer
Iodine (in dropper bottle)	Sun cream
Immodium (or similar for diarrhoea relief)	Lip salve
Dioralyte (or Jeevan Jal for rehydration)	Antiseptic cream
Antibiotic (Ciproxin or as prescribed)	Tiniba (to combat *giardia*)
Scissors	Safety pins

Also recommended is a pack of sterile needles for use in emergencies where injections are necessary, in order to reduce the risk of accidental transmission of HIV (AIDS) and Hepatitis B viruses through contaminated equipment. MASTA (see above) produces a sterile medical equipment pack that contains syringes, sutures and dressings as well as needles.

A copy of *The Himalayan First Aid Manual* by Jim Duff and Peter Gormly, available from KEEP in Kathmandu, is also well worth carrying. It is a slim, pocket-sized manual packed with valuable information.

Most medicines, including antibiotics, are readily available without prescription in Kathmandu (general pharmacies are located on New Road and in various parts of Thamel). Do not rely on the diagnostic advice of untrained pharmacists (some are well qualified, though); where doubts occur seek medical assistance. Make sure you have all you might be expected to require in the way of medical aid before setting out on trek.

More detailed medical advice and preparation may be gleaned from reading James A. Wilkerson's *Medicine for Mountaineering* (The Mountaineers), or Peter Steele's *Medical Handbook for Mountaineers* (Constable).

MAPS

In third world countries, mapping is at best erratic and imprecise.
(The Adventure Travel Handbook)

That quotation could be true of many regions of Nepal, but as the area covered by this guidebook contains the highest mountain on earth, it is certainly not apt here. As Ed Hillary once said of the Khumbu, it is 'the most surveyed, examined, blood-taken, anthropologically dissected area in the world'. The map-makers have been busy.

The best coverage, beautifully drawn and produced on 'trek-proof' paper to a scale of 1:50,000, is the four-colour series published by Freytag-Berndt in Vienna, generally known as the Schneider maps after cartographer Erwin Schneider who undertook the initial fieldwork. Their quality is outstanding, a quality that is reflected in their price. They are stocked by Stanfords in London and The Map

Shop, Upton-upon Severn, and are sometimes available in Kathmandu.

Three sheets deal with the Jiri to Everest route. *Tamba Kosi* includes the trail from Jiri to Junbesi, *Shorong/Hinku* deals with Junbesi to Namche, and *Khumbu Himal* covers all the country north of Namche included in this guide. The same publisher also produces a more detailed sheet at a scale of 1:25,000 which concentrates on Mount Everest and its immediate environs.

In 1988 the National Geographic Society in Washington DC published their own high quality map of Mount Everest at a scale of 1:50,000. Although it may have little practical trekking value (it concentrates as much on the Tibetan side of the mountain as it does the Nepalese, and spreads as far south only as Pangboche and Ama Dablam), it is one of the most accurate sheets ever produced of the Everest region and serves well as a souvenir of the trek to it. This map is generally on sale in Kathmandu bookshops.

Of an entirely different standard, Mandala Productions cover the whole Jiri to Everest route in a single dyeline sheet at a scale of 1:110,000. In the 'Latest Trekking Map' series, the sheet to look for is titled *Lamosangu to Mt Everest & Solu-Khumbu*. Although woefully lacking in meaningful contours, and with a number of inaccuracies, it is perfectly adequate for general day-to-day use along the trail. But if you want to identify peaks as you trek you'll need the Schneider maps mentioned above.

GETTING THERE

For many people distant places have a peculiar form of magnetism which grows as the distance increases. (H.W. Tilman)

By Air:

Eight international airlines fly to Nepal, and those linking Europe with Tribhuvan International Airport, Kathmandu, include the following:

Royal Nepal Airlines Corporation (RNAC), Biman Bangladesh Airlines, Pakistan International Airlines (PIA), and Lufthansa.

Royal Nepal operate twice-weekly flights from London, calling at

Frankfurt and Dubai. They become heavily booked in advance of the main trekking seasons, so plan well ahead if you hope to travel with them. Royal Nepal also arrange charter flights.

Flights by Biman and PIA necessitate making connections in Dhaka and Karachi respectively. Biman currently offer the cheapest tickets, but be warned that on occasion an unannounced delay of 24 hours or more can leave passengers frustrated in Dhaka. Lufthansa flies direct from Frankfurt to Kathmandu.

Other flights may be arranged that require connections via India. Unfortunately the bureaucracy involved in organising transit at Delhi Airport can be somewhat tedious.

Flights out of Kathmandu are nearly always completely booked during the main trekking seasons. It is essential to reconfirm homeward flights at least 72 hours before departure time. Failure to do so may lead to the loss of your seat and you will then have plenty of time to regret the omission. The safest bet is to reconfirm as soon as you arrive in Kathmandu, and reconfirm once more on your return from trek. Before spending the last of your Nepalese currency, check the amount of departure tax to be paid at the airport. The precise amount depends on your destination.

By Other Means:

Trekkers heading for Nepal from India will find that a combination of rail and road travel will take about 3 days for the journey from Delhi to Kathmandu by way of Agra, Varanasi, Patna and the border crossing at Birganj. Coming from Darjeeling it is possible to take an Indian train to Siliguri, and taxi from there to the border post at Kakar Bhitta which has a bus service to Biratnagar in eastern Nepal. Buses and internal aircraft ply the journey from Biratnagar to Kathmandu.

Entering by road from Tibet is by way of Kodari, but this crossing is often closed by landslide during the monsoon.

All vehicles entering Nepal must have an international *carnet de passage*.

Travel Within Nepal:

Domestic flights are operated by RNAC, Nepal Airways, and one or two other independent airlines. All flights by foreigners must be paid for in US dollars. Of particular interest to trekkers planning to visit

47

Solu-Khumbu are the STOL airstrips at Phaplu and Lukla; there is another above Namche at Syangboche that is used by charter flights, mostly for clients of the Everest View Hotel, but as its altitude is 3900m (12,795ft) flying there from Kathmandu is to risk severe mountain sickness on arrival.

Lukla is the busiest STOL (Short Take-Off and Landing) airstrip in Nepal, with a mixed reputation. Some love the excitement of flying into (or out of) this bumpy, sloping strip of hillside above the Dudh Kosi, while others are terrified. Pieces of wrecked fuselage alongside the runway do little to inspire confidence. Stories abound of angry crowds of trekkers being stranded here for several days because low cloud effectively prevented aircraft from getting in. On occasion helicopters are flown in to ease the situation, but the cost of a seat on one of these is exorbitant.

If you wish to fly, and have the necessary time, Phaplu below Junbesi offers an alternative to Lukla, with better opportunities to acclimatise as you walk in towards the high mountains of Khumbu.

Taxis are cheap to use in and around the Kathmandu valley, and are ideal for sightseeing purposes. It can often be worth hiring a taxi for a whole day (agree a price first), especially if you plan to visit a number of different sites.

Public buses provide an 'interesting' and very cheap way to travel in Nepal. Invariably overcrowded, discomfort is guaranteed as the seats are designed with the Nepalese in mind, who as a race are generally several inches shorter than Europeans. Occasionally seats have a bit of padding; often they don't. On a long journey it is virtually certain that several passengers will be overcome by travel sickness and watch the miles pass by throwing up out of the windows. Although against the law to do so, it is often more comfortable to spend the journey on the rooftop with piles of baggage.

Public buses serve Jiri from Kathmandu, a journey of 188 kilometres (117 miles) that takes something like 9-11 hours, including a *daal bhat* stop at Lamosangu. At Charikot foreigners must register at a police check-post.

As an alternative way of reaching Jiri for the trek to Everest, rather than by air or public bus, it may be worth hiring a car or mini-bus with a driver. Several agents in Kathmandu can provide this service - but be prepared to haggle for a reasonable price. It may help to shop around. Travel by private vehicle allows you to stop whenever you choose, and is useful for keen photographers. You'll also arrive in Jiri several hours earlier than you would by bus, and feeling much less exhausted too.

NEPAL - FACTS AND FIGURES

The whole of Nepal is like a pretty woman, with a blush ever ready to erupt. (The Times of India)

Rectangular in shape and measuring roughly 800 kilometres by 240 (500 miles by 150), Nepal contains the largest number of 8000m (26,000ft) peaks in the world. But mountains form only the northern part of this beautiful country. In the south is the tropical belt of the Terai - an extension of the Gangetic plain - while the broad central region is one of fertile hills rising from 600 to 2000m (2000-6500ft) in altitude. The sub-tropical Kathmandu valley is included in this central strip, as are neighbouring valley basins.

It is the world's only Hindu monarchy. Officially some 90% of the population of about 18 million are said to be Hindu, and just 8% of the Buddhist faith, but Hinduism and Buddhism merge compatibly in so many different ways here that it is not always easy to separate them. When trekking in Solu-Khumbu one sees more evidence of Buddhism than any other faith, and it is partly due to the spirituality of the local people that the area is so appealing. Since Buddhists are more tolerant of outsiders than are Hindus, one has several opportunities to visit monasteries and other religious structures along the way.

The official language, Nepali, is derived from Pahori which comes from northern India and is spoken by some 58% of the population. But it has been said that there are as many different languages in Nepal as there are races, and as many dialects as there are villages. In the Kathmandu valley the original language of Newari uses no less than three different alphabets. Fortunately for the Western trekker English is widely understood in Kathmandu and in most lodges along the popular trails, and most Sherpas who generally make up the crew of organised treks also speak a modicum of English - while the more educated among them often learn smatterings of other European languages too.

49

Although it numbers among the six poorest nations on earth in terms of per capita income, the trekker in Nepal does not experience the same sense of hopeless poverty that is so prevalent in a number of other Eastern countries. The majority of its population depend for their livelihood on agriculture, much of which is subsistence farming on the intricate terraced fields that create such an artistic picture on the hillsides. Some 17% of land is under cultivation, and about 30% covered by forest. However, while Nepal was self-sufficient in food production in the early 1950s, the demands of a fast-growing population and a corresponding increase in livestock has seen that self-sufficiency fade to one of grain-deficiency and a marked reduction in forests. Nepal now faces serious economic and environmental problems which only considered development can arrest.

Some experts forecast a doom-laden future by virtue of the shrinking forests and the subsequent speeding of hillside erosion. Others point to the fact that the Himalaya is a young mountain range, still growing, and suggest that deforestation is not so bad as is depicted. In his *Travels in Nepal*, Charlie Pye-Smith makes the following comment: 'Depending on which pair of estimates you take, you can show that a) the Himalaya will be washed down to the Bay of Bengal next week; b) the mountains will sink under the weight of vegetation; c) something between these two extremes is happening'.

Tourism is the largest source of income (only 2% of labour is employed in industry), and trekking provides much needed foreign currency essential to the country's development, although at present Nepal relies very heavily on foreign aid programmes for major development projects - some of which may be questionable in the light of problems hinted at above. (*Travels in Nepal* provides an interesting commentary on the question of foreign aid here.)

International telecommunication is possible through the British earth satellite station installed in 1982. Telephone connections with Europe and the United States are good, and are widely available in Kathmandu. A number of hotels and trekking agencies in the capital now have fax facilities.

Nepalese time is 5 hours 45 minutes ahead of Greenwich Mean Time (15 minutes ahead of Indian Standard Time; 13 hours 45 minutes ahead of Pacific Time, USA, and 10 hours 45 minutes ahead of US Eastern Time).

Postal services are dealt with in Kathmandu at the General Post Office located at the junction of Kantipath and Kicha-Pokhari Road. The office is open daily (except Saturdays and public holidays) from 10.00am to 5.00pm (4.00pm November to February). When posting always ensure that stamps on postcards, letters or parcels are franked by the counter clerk. There is invariably a queue at the special counter reserved for franking stamps. Several villages along the trail to Everest have Post Offices of some description. Postcards and letters may be sent from these, and mostly they get delivered - often long after you've returned home from trek.

The currency of Nepal is the rupee (rps) which is made up of 100 paisa. As a 'soft' currency it should not be taken out of the country (it has no exchange value outside Nepal). Travellers cheques and 'hard' currency can be exchanged at Tribhuvan Airport on arrival (make sure you are given the correct amount of rupees), and at a number of banks which are open daily, except Saturdays, from 10.00am until about 2.00pm. Always collect your exchange receipts as these may be needed when applying for trekking permits or visa extensions. Make a point of accumulating plenty of small-denomination notes for use on trek. It is no good stopping at a trailside tea-house a week's walk from the nearest bank and expect to pay for your cup of tea with a Rps 500 or Rps 1000 note.

TIME IN KATHMANDU

And the wildest dreams of Kew are the facts of Kathmandu.
(Rudyard Kipling)

Kathmandu is one of the world's most magical cities and it is worth devoting a few days, either before or after trek, to absorbing its unique atmosphere and exploring neighbouring towns within the valley. After weeks among the mountains it is a great place to sample a change of menu, too, for there are dozens of restaurants to satisfy all appetites. There are numerous hotels and guest-houses of varying degrees of comfort, and enough shops and street traders offering a thousand and one 'bargains' to help you spend the last of your money.

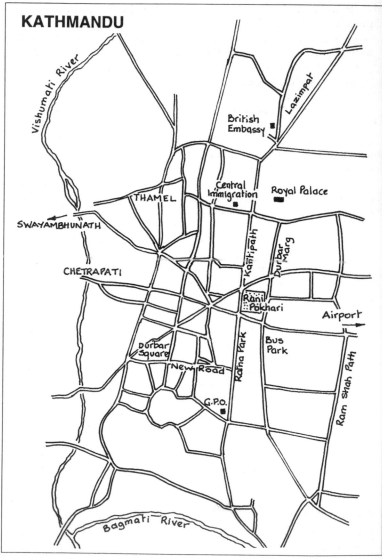

In the 1870s David Wright, a surgeon at the British Residency, produced a report which cynics might consider apt today. It read: 'The streets of Kathmandu are very narrow, mere lanes in fact; and the whole town is very dirty...to clean the drains would be impossible without knocking down the entire city...In short, from a sanitary point of view, Kathmandu may be said to be built on a dunghill in the middle of latrines'.

That is but one view. Kathmandu is a cornucopia of colour, of smells, of noise. It *is* dirty, but it's also exciting, vibrant. A dull cloud of pollution hangs over the city, but below it there's unbridled gaiety, and in countless streets medieval buildings are adorned with carvings of delicate beauty. There are people everywhere, the narrow alleyways and broad modern roads acrush with activity. Traffic streams in an endless honking procession through the daylight hours along its main highways. Bicycle rickshaws and taxis bounce and weave through the teeming streets of Thamel, and manage somehow to avoid collision with crowds of traders, the bustle of porters, tourists and beggars, and the occasional cow.

Thamel, the ever-popular district in the north-west of the city, has a plentiful supply of budget accommodation in small hotels and guest-houses, a fine selection of restaurants and bookshops, suppliers of climbing and trekking equipment, outfitters of all kinds, and a specialist trekker's food shop. If your airline has sent your baggage to Honolulu by mistake, you'll find all you need in the shops of Thamel.

Its wealth of religious and cultural sites makes Kathmandu extraordinarily appealing. 'There are nearly as many temples as houses, and as many idols as inhabitants' wrote W. Kirkpatrick in 1811, and while there are certainly more houses and inhabitants today, plus a great number of tourists, there is no shortage of places to visit. The following suggestions merely scratch the surface. For more detailed information, background history and a pointer to the full glories of the valley itself, the *Insight Guide: Nepal* (APA Publications) is highly recommended.

Kathmandu:

Durbar Square is a must. Dominated by the Taleju Temple it contains more than 50 important monuments, shrines and temples, as well as

Buddhist pilgrims make their devotions as they circle the great stupa at Swayambhunath

the Hanuman Dhoka (Royal Palace), and offers a superb roofscape of exotic shapes. Intricate carvings adorn every building: figures, faces, patterns and religious symbols by the metre on struts and beams, and around doorways and windows. Early morning is the best time to visit. Street vendors are setting out their wares, porters gather to await employment, the faithful scurry to various temples for their first devotions of the day, and the place comes alive with streams of light, colour and movement. By mid-morning the Square is crowded.

North-east of the city, a short taxi ride away, **Bodhnath's** dome, 40m (130ft) high, makes it the largest Buddhist stupa in all Nepal. Seen from afar it is the country's centre of Tibetan culture. Monasteries and pilgrim rest-houses cluster around, and at the start of the Tibetan New Year monks take part in colourful ceremonies here. Masked dances are performed for the public in a nearby field, while other dances take place in a monastery courtyard.

On a site considered sacred more than 2500 years ago, the great stupa of **Swayambhunath** looks down on the city from its hilltop perch to the west of the Vishumati river. A long flight of steps leads

The Vishumati river flows round the western edge of Kathmandu and separates the city from farmland

to it among trees where monkeys play, and from the top a grand view overlooks the valley. A row of prayer wheels encircles the stupa, and behind it a gompa, or monastery, attracts visitors. Inside hundreds of butter lamps flicker while drums, gongs and trumpets accompany each devotion.

The Vishumati flows round the western side of Kathmandu, while the Bagmati twists along the eastern boundary and is bordered by **Pashupatinath**, the largest Hindu shrine in Nepal. As a tributary of the Ganges the Bagmati is considered sacred by devout Hindus. Overlooking it a temple complex is forbidden to non-Hindus, but on the east bank a series of terraces provide viewpoints from which to study not only the gilded temple, but also riverside activities below. In the river women do their laundry; others take part in ritual bathing, while Hindus fast approaching death are lain on stone slabs with their feet in the water until all life has drained from them. Nearby ghats are used by commoners for cremation, others are reserved for the use of royalty.

Patan:

South of Kathmandu, and divided from it only by the Bagmati river, Patan is a very old town founded, it is claimed, in the third century BC by the emperor Ashoka and his daughter Carumati. Primarily a Buddhist town it has around 150 former monasteries, but there are also many Hindu temples and shrines and scores of exotic buildings, so that it would take weeks of study to properly visit each one.

This 'town of a thousand golden roofs' has its own **Durbar Square** with the one-time Royal Palace facing a complex variety of Newari architectural wonders. The Palace itself has three main courtyards open to the public, each displaying the skills of woodcarvers of past generations. Nearby the beautiful Kva Bahal, or Golden Temple, dates from the twelfth century.

Like Kathmandu, Patan is a bustling town but with a vibrancy all its own. When you've absorbed as much spiritual and architectural wonder as you can, stroll among the bazaars and enjoy haggling for bargains with the street vendors.

Bhaktapur:

Also known by its former name of Bhadgaon, this handsome town of about 50,000 lies 16 kilometres (10 miles) to the east of Kathmandu. The journey is a pleasant one, for it travels through open country and then climbs among pine trees and alongside two small reservoirs on the outskirts of the town itself.

Badly damaged in 1934 by an earthquake that also devastated the capital, Bhaktapur nevertheless retains much of its medieval character and is in many respects the finest in the valley with regard to architectural delights. Much of the restoration work has been made possible through a German-Nepalese development project that has so far helped preserve some 200 buildings without destroying their essential character. The best is in **Durbar Square** which is entered through a gateway. There you find a broad open approach to a magnificent collection of temples and monuments. At least two large temples were completely destroyed by the earthquake, but those that remain are set out with sufficient space to enable the visitor to study them from different angles without their being confused among other crowded buildings.

Whilst Durbar Square is the main focus of attention in Bhaktapur, a short stroll leads to **Taumadhi Square**, surrounded by lovely old Newari houses and dominated by the Nyatapola Temple, Bhaktapur's largest. In the Tachupal quarter is **Dattatraya Square** with its own fifteenth-century temple and a lively atmosphere. Linked by narrow alleyways there is much to explore. Take particular note of the magnificent carvings that adorn so many buildings, especially round windows and doorways. The art of the woodcarver here has reached the very height of perfection.

The Treks

The body roams the mountains, and the spirit is set free.

(Hsu Hsia-k'o)

THE TRAIL TO EVEREST

Prior to the outbreak of the Second World War all expeditions to Everest had to approach the mountain through Tibet as Nepal was firmly closed to foreigners. But by the early 1950s the situation was reversed. Tibet was effectively closed by the Chinese invasion, and at the same time the doors to the once-forbidden kingdom of Nepal had slowly begun to open.

A party of Indian scientists had gained permission to enter the Khumbu in 1948, and in 1950 the first Westerners were given leave to explore the southern approaches to Mount Everest. The Indian party climbed to the trading pass of the Nangpa La on the Tibetan border west of Cho Oyu, but it was the small, privately organised group (hardly an expedition) led by the American Dr Charles Houston, who first reached the Khumbu glacier below Everest itself. With Houston was the legendary mountaineer-explorer Bill Tilman, who had already been on two pre-war Everest expeditions, and who was now eager for an opportunity to study the mountain from the unknown south and west.

Their route of approach began, not in Kathmandu, but way off to the south-east in Dharan. At first they followed the Arun river north towards Makalu before striking roughly westward across successive ridges that eventually brought them to the Dudh Kosi below Lukla. By the time they reached Chaumrikharka they had joined the main trail used by the majority of trekkers today, and followed it upvalley to Namche Bazaar and beyond, as far as the Khumbu glacier and the slopes of Kala Pattar.

Houston and Tilman's route is still used today, although it is much less frequented than either the direct flight to Lukla, or the long approach from the roadhead at Jiri.

Following Houston and Tilman's visit, and a reconnaissance led by Eric Shipton, a Swiss expedition made the first attempt to climb Mount Everest from Nepal in 1952. Their route of approach began in the Kathmandu valley and took 23 days, including two rest days in Namche. Next, in the spring of 1953, came the successful British expedition under John Hunt's leadership, and they took basically the same route pioneered by the Swiss. In the wake of his team's success Hunt's book, *The Ascent of Everest*, proved enormously popular, as did the film made by Tom Stobart which enjoyed a wide distribution. Together they made a huge impression on a generation of would-be mountaineers and fired the imagination of countless armchair adventurers who were excited not only by the success of Hillary and Tenzing in gaining the summit, but by the sheer beauty of the landscapes leading to the mountain itself.

Trekking, as it is known today, was subsequently 'invented' by mountaineer and former Ghurka officer Jimmy Roberts, who rightly guessed that tourists would jump at the chance to follow in the footsteps of Hunt, Hillary, Tenzing and Co through those glorious valleys, would not only enjoy but pay for the privilege of sleeping in tents among such staggering scenery, and walk by day in the company of the fabled Sherpas with porters to carry their equipment and food. Not surprisingly, the first commercial trek ever organised in Nepal led across the foothills and along the valley of the Dudh Kosi towards Mount Everest.

Soon the country was sprouting roads like unruly tendrils of bindweed. By the time the Chinese-built highway that now goes to Tibet had reached Lamosangu in 1970, the approach walk to Everest had been reduced in length by several days. Now a spur, built under Swiss direction, has reached Jiri from Lamosangu, thus making it possible to trek to Kala Pattar in considerably less than a fortnight from the roadhead. While the walk-in is maybe ten days shorter than the Swiss took in 1952, once the road has been left behind the route is much the same, except the Swiss had to make a diversion over the Lumding La because the bridge over the Dudh Kosi below Manidingma had been washed away. Today's route is full of variety and considerable charm, but not without an awful lot of height gain and loss. Anyone expecting an easy but persistent incline from Jiri to Namche is in for a shock.

With the construction of an airstrip to Lukla, the long walk-in from the foothills has been overtaken in popularity by a much shorter approach. From Lukla, Namche is less than 2 days' easy walk away, and is therefore within the range of most people's holiday allocation. It is now possible to walk to the base of Everest and out again in less than a fortnight.

As set out in the following pages, the trek to Everest is described in several different sections. The first deals with the walk-in from Jiri to Namche Bazaar, and includes the most heavily trekked section from Lukla. At Namche it will be necessary to take a rest day or two in order to aid acclimatisation, and suggested walks are given for this.

Then comes the walk through the Sherpa heartland of Khumbu from Namche Bazaar to Lobuche, Gorak Shep and Kala Pattar, with a side trip via Dingboche to Chhukhung below the great wall of Lhotse.

Next is described the splendid trek that branches away from the main valley just above Namche, and visits the sparkling lakes of Gokyo in the ablation trough beside Nepal's largest glacier, followed by outline suggestions for other treks in the shadow of the world's highest mountain.

Although the various routes which follow are set out in day stages, these are merely offered as a rough guide for ease of planning. It is not necessary for independent travellers to stick rigidly to this plan. Indeed, it would be unfortunate if everyone adhered to the same itinerary, for in that way certain lodges would become horribly overcrowded while others fell into disuse. As approximate timings for the various stages are frequently given in the following pages, as well as a note of villages where accommodation is available throughout, it should be possible to create your own itinerary based on information provided. On an organised group trek, of course, the sirdar and leader will have their own favoured places to halt for the night, thus creating a different plan again.

One final word on the choice of lodges. There is a homing instinct among large numbers of independent trekkers who, seeing one particular lodge being patronised by Westerners, will automatically choose that one too, while the place next door, which may be identical in every other respect - or even better in some - remains empty. Unless there's a very good reason for doing otherwise, please spread the load, thus giving all the lodges an equal share of business. Tea-house trekking helps stimulate the local economy, and the few rupees you spend in a particular lodge or shop can have a positive effect. You may gain additional benefits, too, for in a less busy lodge there's an opportunity to witness the daily life of a Sherpa family and, if you're sensitive to other cultures, learn much from it.

Houses in Lamosangu back onto the Sun Kosi. It is here that the road to Jiri leaves the Chinese-built Kodari highway (P67)

ROUTE SUMMARIES

Route	Distance	Height gain/loss		Time	Page
Jiri to Namche Bazaar					
1: Kathmandu-Jiri	188kms			1 day	66
2: Jiri-Shivalaya	8kms	495m	(-600m)	3-3½hrs	68
3: Shivalaya-Bhandar	8km	905m	(-511m)	4-4½hrs	70
4: Bhandar-Sete	10kms	1032m	(-651m)	6-6½hrs	72
5: Sete-Junbesi	12kms	955m	(-855m)	6-6½hrs	74
6: Junbesi-Manidingma	14kms	845m	(-1326m)	6-7hrs	78
7: Manidingma-Kharikhola	8kms	579m	(-701m)	4hrs	80
8: Kharikhola-Chaumrikharka	14kms	1191m	(-550m)	8hrs	83
8a: Lukla-Choplung	3kms		(-200m)	30mins-1hr	87
9: Chaumrikharka-Mondzo	10kms	410m	(-314m)	4-4½hrs	87
10: Mondzo-Namche Bazaar	5kms	611m		3-3½hrs	90
11-12:Acclimatisation days in Namche Bazaar					
Namche Bazaar to Lobuche, Gorak Shep and Kala Pattar					
1: Namche-Thyangboche	19kms	771m	(-350m)	4-4½hrs	100
2: Thyangboche-Pheriche	10kms	502m	(-87m)	4-4½hrs	104
Thyangboche-Dingboche	10kms	563m	(-87m)	4-4½hrs	106
3: Acclimatisation day in Pheriche or Dingboche					
4: Pheriche-Lobuche	8kms	678m		3-4hrs	111
Dingboche-Lobuche	9.5kms	587m		3-4hrs	113
5: Lobuche-Gorak Shep-Kala Pattar	6kms	693m		4-4½hrs	114
Namche Bazaar to Gokyo					
1: Namche-Dole	10kms	1004m	(-366m)	5-6hrs	125
2: Dole-Machhermo	4.5kms	381m		2-2½hrs	128
3: Machhermo-Gokyo	7kms	326m		3-3½hrs	130

JIRI TO NAMCHE BAZAAR

From the foothills to the foot of the high mountains, this first half of the trek involves the crossing of a series of ridges separated by deep river valleys. It's a corrugated route, for the main ridges - long arthritic fingers of land - project southward while the trail heads east across them. Between the ridges glacial rivers pour down to the valley of the Sun Kosi that flows at right-angles through eastern Nepal. As Jiri lies west of the Dudh Kosi, the river that drains Khumbu, it follows that in order to reach this valley there's no alternative but to head across the grain of the land. Only when the Dudh Kosi has been gained can the trek assume its longed-for direction - upvalley towards the north, towards Namche Bazaar and Everest itself.

The first few days, then, are energetic days; climbing out of warm river valleys, up terraced hillsides, through forest and over high crests with far views to enjoy, then steeply down again to the next river, milky-blue with glacier-melt. Despite much height gain after leaving Jiri, at the point of crossing the Dudh Kosi several days later you're more than 400m (1300ft) lower than when you started! Thereafter the trail heads upvalley, mostly along steep hillsides maintaining an up-and-down regime where mountain spurs intervene, but less severely than before.

Some fine lodges are dotted along the trail, as well as one or two interesting villages. Hillsides are often clothed with a wide range of vegetation fed by the heavy rains of summer - eastern Nepal receiving more of the monsoon's annual downpour than almost any other part of the Himalaya - and in the foothills and middle hills agricultural terraces provide a constant patchwork of delight, and are immensely photogenic.

As the majority of inhabitants of Solu-Khumbu are Buddhists you will pass a great number of mani walls, chortens and stupas, each of which should be passed on its left-hand side. These structures hold great significance. A *chorten* may appear to be just a pile of stones with prayer flags sprouting from it, but it is a stylized representation of Buddha. A *stupa* is far more elaborately symbolic; its base denotes the

ROUTE PROFILE: JIRI TO NAMCHE BAZAAR

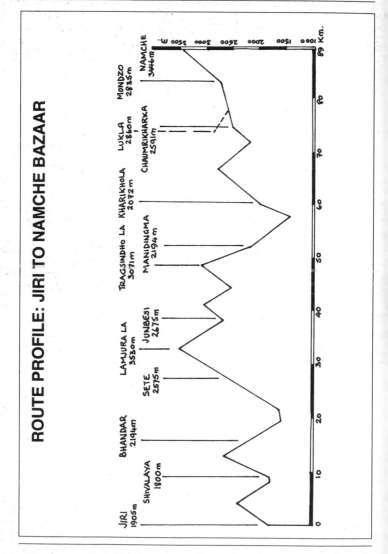

The route crosses the Dudh Kosi by suspension bridge at Phakding

The trekking peak of Kwangde overlooks Namche
Khumjung enjoys a marvellous view of Ama Dablam

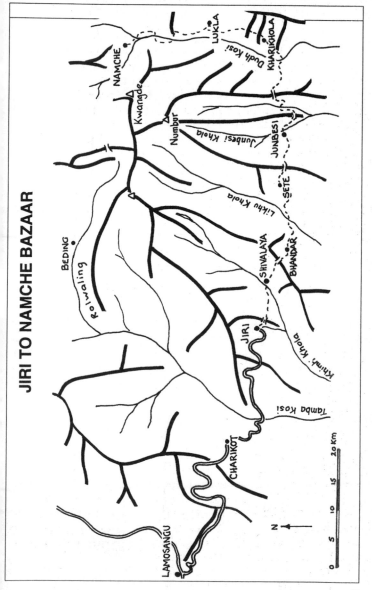

JIRI TO NAMCHE BAZAAR

LUKLA

NAMCHE

KHARIKHOLA

Dudh Kosi

Kwangde

Numbur

Junbesi Khola

JUNBESI

Likhu Khola

SETE

BEDING

Rolwaling

BHANDAR

SHIVALAYA

Khimti Khola

JIRI

Tamba Kosi

CHARIKOT

LAMOSANGU

N

0   5   10   15   20 km

solid earth, the dome above it represents water, while from each side of the rectangular tower above that, a pair of eyes gaze out over the four corners of the earth. Below the eyes of the Buddha is the Sanskrit number one (although it's often mistaken as a nose), painted there to underline the oneness of Buddha. Rising from the rectangular tower is a spire which may be pyramidal or conical, and which is divided by 13 sections (the 13 steps to enlightenment), and finally, on top of all is a spike to symbolise the sacred light of Buddha. Upon *mani stones*, prayer flags and prayer wheels the words '*Om Mani Padme Hum*' (which means 'hail to the jewel in the lotus') are written countless times over. This great mantra, or prayer, when recited over and over again, is an important element in the meditative practice observed by followers of the Buddha. It is one more aspect of life in Solu-Khumbu that adds to the trekker's journey.

KATHMANDU - LAMOSANGU - JIRI

The journey by road from Kathmandu to Jiri is a scenic one. By public bus the 188 kilometres (117 miles) will take a full day; a bone-numbing epic of anything up to 12 hours that will have you yearning for the freedom of the trail long before the nightmare ends at the roadhead. As far as Lamosangu the road is in a poor condition and buses either crash over and through the potholes, or weave a slalom course around them. Once across the iron bridge over the Sun Kosi river, however, the surface improves to Swiss standards and those who are riding on the roof of the bus (illegal but popular) can begin to enjoy the views. As mentioned earlier, some may wish to forego the dubious pleasures of ethnic travel and hire a private vehicle for the journey.

Buses bound for Jiri depart from the main bus park east of Tundikhel in Kathmandu in the early morning and are invariably overcrowded. Heading along the Chinese-built Kodari Highway the route makes for Bhaktapur, then climbs out of the valley to Dhulikhel. From the ridge crest in the cool of morning views can be quite stunning from here, with a long serrated horizon of big mountains showing as an extension of the clouds.

The road descends to the Indrawati, then follows it to Dolalaghat where a bridge crosses the river. Beyond this the road climbs over another ridge before tracking the Sun Kosi ('Gold River') upstream to **LAMOSANGU** (78 kilometres: 49 miles) where a scheduled stop gives just enough time for a plate of *daal bhat* before the bus sets off again on the next stage.

Lamosangu is a scruffy little town astride the Chinese road, about 50 kilometres (31 miles) south of the Tibetan border. Some of the houses stand perilously close to the water's edge, being built on the very bank of the Sun Kosi. Here the bus breaks away to the right, crosses the river on a large iron bridge, and then begins a long, sinuous climb among a range of hills with another 110 kilometres to go before reaching Jiri. From now on the road surface is much improved, thanks to a Swiss aid project that has made it the finest highway in all Nepal. (Although financed and engineered by the Swiss, it was at the outset planned to be labour-intensive, and at one time some 9000 Nepalese labourers were employed on its construction. The road took 11 years to build.)

Halfway to Jiri the road comes to **CHARIKOT** (131 kilometres: 81 miles) where there is a police check-post and trekking permit details need to be entered in a logbook. Among a skyline of mountains seen from here the double-pronged Gaurishankar (7145m: 23,441ft) towers above its neighbours of the Rolwaling Himal. Charikot (or nearby Dolakha) is often used as the starting point for treks into Rolwaling, thus providing an alternative route to Khumbu by way of the difficult and potentially dangerous pass of the Trashi Labtsa. The turn-off for Dolakha, which has some interesting temples, is opposite the police check-post.

Below Charikot the road crosses the Tamba Kosi just north of its confluence with the Charnawati Khola, then rises again over more foothills to top a ridge at about 2500m (8200ft). There is one more police check-post at Jiri Bazaar, then the bus continues its downhill run, makes a left-hand bend, and the township of Jiri is seen just ahead, its cluster of lodges and houses set in a lush, fertile basin backed by wooded hills.

JIRI (1905m: 6250ft) is more attractive, and a lot tidier, than some other roadhead townships in Nepal. On either side of the road a number of lodges and shops provide a service for trekkers, both at the start and end of their treks. On arrival a few touts gather round claiming, of course, that their lodge is 'best in town'. In truth there's probably not a lot between any of them. A camping area will be found near the entrance to the main street, on the left-hand side of the road.

Jiri has received a lot of attention from the Swiss who centred a number of development projects on the town. Not only did they build the road from Lamosangu, but also set up a cheese factory, and helped establish a technical school, hospital and an agricultural station as part of the Jiri Multi-purpose Development Project (JMDP). (Charlie Pye-Smith's book *Travels in Nepal* discusses the successes and failures of these, and other, aid schemes, and makes interesting background reading.)

JIRI - SHIVALAYA

Distance:	8 kilometres (5 miles)
Time:	3-3¹/₂ hours
Start altitude:	1905m (6250ft)
High point:	Patashe Danda (2400m: 7874ft)
Height gain:	495m (1624ft)
Descent:	600m (1968ft)
Accommodation:	Lodges in Mali and Shivalaya

The first stage of any trek in Nepal has its own indefinable quality. Following a long road journey, such as that from Kathmandu to Jiri, one longs for the peace and tranquillity of the hills, becomes restless and eager for physical exercise after being cramped in an overcrowded bus for many numbing hours. For those on a group trek the first day's walk will necessarily be a short one as porters have to be organised by the sirdar, and by the time that's accomplished the morning will be well advanced.

Before the road reached Jiri in 1984 the standard trekking route did not come here at all, but passed through Those, a one-time industrial centre and bazaar town down-valley beside the Khimti Khola. Since the coming of the road to Jiri Those has fallen into decline, and the route to it become less popular than before. Some trekkers still choose that traditional way, however, which makes a slightly longer route than the one described below.

This stage is described as ending at Shivalaya, for that's where many groups settle their first camp. Independent trekkers may find they have time and energy to continue as far as Sangbadanda or Deorali, described on the way to Bhandar under the next section.

On the trek to Shivalaya a pleasant, undemanding climb leads to a ridge-crest where the first view of distant snowpeaks may be seen across a succession of foothill ridges. Descent on the south-eastern side of this crest eventually leads into the valley of the Khimti Khola, a descent that is more tiring than the ascent on account of the steepness of the slope below Mali.

At the end of the road in Jiri there's an open area where buses park overnight. A broad and obvious trail breaks away from this and heads along the left-hand side of the valley. In 10 minutes cross a stream, just beyond which the trail forks. Bear left and begin winding up the wooded hillside for a further 15 minutes, emerging onto a saddle with a few simple shacks and tea-houses astride the trail. This is **BHARKUR** (*refreshments*). Now out in the open the path continues high along the hillside on a charming belvedere above terraced fields, climbs a little and, 20 minutes from Bharkur, comes to the school and few houses of **RATMATE** (*refreshments*).

Continue climbing steadily and, about 1 hour 15 minutes from Jiri, the trail brings you to **CHITRE** (*refreshments*), a small cluster of tea-houses perched on an open hillside. Beyond this the way leads across an area of shrubs, edges alongside pinewoods (fine foothill views to enjoy), and then tops the crest of a ridge. Off to the left the horizon is a jagged line of great snowpeaks.

In a little over 1¹/₂ hours from Jiri you will come to a small pass on the **PATASHE DANDA** (2400m: 7874ft) marked with prayer flags. Just below, 5 minutes or so away, the first buildings of Mali can be seen. Descend on a trail that slopes down the left-hand side of the ridge, and come to a tea-house. The rest of **MALI** (*accommodation, refreshments*) is strung out below, with lodges, more tea-houses and a school.

From here the trail continues to descend into the valley of the Yelung Khola, but quite steeply now, and care will be required after rain. Several primitive tea-houses line the way. Soon after passing **DOVAN**, cross to the left bank of the Yelung Khola by way of a bridge, and wander down towards the main valley which crosses at right-angles ahead. Shivalaya is seen as you turn the hillside into the Khimti Khola valley. Pass a solitary lodge, then cross a suspension bridge into the unpretentious village of **SHIVALAYA** (1800m: 5905ft), reached about 1¹/₂ hours from Mali.

The lodges and shops of Shivalaya are built in a line facing one another across a single street. The water supply for the village is found just to the right at the end of the bridge (remember to treat all water for drinking), and the camping area is also off to the right beyond the lodges. A police check-post is situated at the far end of the village where trekking permits will need to be examined.

SHIVALAYA - DEORALI - BHANDAR

Distance:	8 kilometres (5 miles)
Time:	4-4¹/₂ hours
Start altitude:	1800 metres (5905ft)
High point:	Deorali (2705m: 8875ft)
Height gain:	905 metres (2970ft)
Descent:	511 metres (1677ft)
Accommodation:	Lodges in Sangbadanda, Deorali and Bhandar

Although the basic linear distance between Shivalaya and Bhandar is not great, the trail makes additional demands on account of height gain. This is not excessive either, on paper, but the initial uphill section out of Shivalaya will be quite steep enough for trekkers not yet in Himalaya mode.

Before leaving Shivalaya it will be necessary to provide details of your trekking permit at the police check-post. Just beyond this the path curves left to cross first a small stream, then a suspension bridge over a larger stream where there are more houses with alpine views to mountains that crowd the head of the Khimti Khola valley. The trail now begins a steep climb up the hillside on a series of stone slab steps. In about 15 minutes you leave the shade of trees and come to a group of simple tea-shacks (*refreshments*) overlooking lush terraces on the opposite hills, and the broad, stony river bed below.

In a little over another hour you come to the small scattered village of **SANGBADANDA** (2240m: 7349ft, 1¹/₂ hours, *accommodation, refreshments*) which has a school and a few lodges strung along the trail. About 2 minutes after passing the last building the trail forks.

Both options lead eventually to the crest-top village of Deorali and are outlined below.

Standard Route to Deorali:

The main trail is the right-hand option. At first it makes a delightful contour round the hillside, passes a few houses, then climbs in fits and starts, broken with more level sections and crossing a number of minor streams. Several tea-houses are found along the way. Much of the route leads through woodland, and the final climb to Deorali is among a forest of rhododendrons. By this route Deorali is reached in about $1^{3}/_{4}$ hours from Sangbadanda.

High Trail via Thodung:

The left-hand trail just beyond Sangbadanda climbs to the ridge at **THODUNG** (3091m: 10,141ft) by way of Buldanda. This is a longer route than that described above, for it'll take about $2^{1}/_{2}$ hours or so to reach Thodung, and a further hour from there to Deorali where the trails converge. However, this alternative has its advocates. Thodung consists of a lodge, gompa, and a cheese factory, originally set up by the Swiss but now run by the Nepalese Dairy Corporation. From the ridge a fine panorama includes Gaurishankar looming on the northern horizon. From Thodung to Deorali the trail follows the ridge-crest southward.

DEORALI (2705m: 8875ft, 3-3$^{1}/_{2}$ hours by the main route, *accommodation, refreshments*) is a group of lodges clustered on the western side of the ridge that separates the valleys of the Khimti Khola and the Likhu Khola. Running between the lodges is a large mani wall.

Deorali means pass, and with the ridge dipping to a saddle here it is aptly named. Cross over and descend steeply, and in 2 minutes bear left where the trail forks. Bhandar can be seen below, nestling on a broad, sloping hillside shelf. The way to it is quite easy, and in places is paved with stone slabs. There are several mani walls (remember to pass along their left-hand side), and as you come to Bhandar (1 hour 15 minutes from Deorali) you will notice two stupas and a gompa standing within the village, with lodges nearby.

BHANDAR (2194m: 7198ft) has a number of good lodges, one of which (just below the stupas) has a pharmacy attached to it, which could be worth noting. There are two or three possible camping grounds, and a police check-post a little way down the hill from the main grouping of lodges. The village is inhabited by Sherpas, and is situated in a broad slope of meadowland with a few simple terraces nearby. To the east, on the far side of the Likhu Khola valley, rise the hills of the Lamjura Danda onto which the next stage leads.

BHANDAR - KENJA - SETE

Distance:	10 kilometres (6^{1}/$_{2}$ miles)
Time:	6-6$^{1/2}$ hours
Start altitude:	2194m (7198ft)
Low point:	Likhu Khola (1543m: 5062ft)
Descent:	651m (2136ft)
High point:	Sete (2575m: 8448ft)
Height gain:	1032m (3386ft)
Accommodation:	Lodges in Kenja and Sete

Rising to the east of the Likhu Khola the lofty crest of the Lamjura Danda, topped by Pike Peak (4065m: 13,337ft), is the highest obstacle to be crossed on the approach to Namche Bazaar and the Khumbu. This crossing is made at the Lamjura La, a pass nearly 2000m (6500ft) above the river which, for most trekkers who set out from Bhandar, would be too much for one day. The route is therefore usually broken by an overnight at Sete. Fit trekkers who continued the previous stage as far as Kenja, however, may find that an early start for the Lamjura La would give time to get over the pass and down to Junbesi in one long day's trek.

The stage as written below is demanding enough, for although the route down to the valley of the Likhu Khola from Bhandar begins innocently, it soon develops into a sharp, knee-straining descent. The short valley section which leads alongside the river to Kenja may seem a frustrating switchback of an interlude, while the climb to Sete, beginning at Kenja, is unrelentingly steep nearly all the way. But there's plenty of scenic variety to enjoy throughout.

Leaving Bhandar the trail slopes down the broad, fertile hillside, heading between a short avenue of trees and past a number of houses - a charming start to the day. Crossing and recrossing minor streams, about 20 minutes from the upper village you will come to another group of houses and a covered wooden bridge. Cross the bridge and immediately bear left to follow the stream.

The way soon develops as a steep descending path that winds down a heavily vegetated hillside, passing a few simple tea-houses. About 20 minutes from the covered bridge you should reach a group of buildings where the trail then drops very steeply to the left, making towards the bed of the narrow Surma Khola valley.

Soon after drawing level with the Surma Khola the path makes a long contour, the stream then falling far below once more. The trail is obvious, but when you come to a single house, make sure you take the path that descends left, steeply once more.

About $1^{1}/_{2}$ hours after leaving Bhandar cross the Surma Khola on a wooden bridge. On the left bank there are several buildings, a number of them tea-houses. The trail continues down, then curves leftward into the broader valley of the Likhu Khola. Wandering between terraces you will come to a house near a suspension bridge (about 10 minutes from the bridge over the Surma Khola). There is a trail junction. Do not cross the river here, but bear left and continue along the valley path until reaching a second major suspension bridge. Cross to the eastern side where there are a few tea-houses.

The trail maintains direction upvalley and soon becomes something of a switchback all the way to Kenja. The valley is very pleasant with several tea-houses set beside the trail. Eventually you come to yet another suspension bridge. This one straddles a major tributary of the Likhu Khola, across which you enter the lodge settlement of **KENJA** (1634m: 5361ft, 3-3$^{1}/_{2}$ hours, *accommodation, refreshments*). The first building on the left across the bridge is the police check-post. Upvalley an attractive conical snowpeak towers over the river.

Almost immediately upon leaving Kenja the path begins its laborious climb to Sete. It can seem a brutal haul, but with another 3 hours or more to go before reaching the lodges there, it's best to settle to a steady, comfortable rhythm and enjoy the ascent without being tempted to hurry. On occasion views towards the head of the Likhu Khola are very fine as more and more snowpeaks come on display. Then there's the pleasure of gazing steeply down on Kenja and, when that has disappeared from view, Bhandar may be seen way off to the west.

Plenty of tea-houses line the trail, and you'll certainly get through a lot of liquids on this stage, especially if the weather is bright and warm. About 2¹/₂ hours above Kenja there's a lone building by a junction of trails. A sign here indicates that it's not far now to Sete. Be sure to take the left-hand path, climbing steeply once more, but then easing, climbing and easing again until you arrive at a handful of lodges set on brief terraces.

SETE (2575m: 8448ft) is little more than a few lodges and a small gompa perched high above the valley among a series of narrow terraced fields. After the harvest has been taken groups often camp on the terraces beside some of the lodges. There is no immediate water supply here, so the kitchen crew on a group trek, and lodge staff too, have to fetch and carry in large plastic jerrycans from the nearest stream.

SETE - LAMJURA LA - JUNBESI

Distance:	12 kilometres (7¹/₂ miles)
Time:	6-6¹/₂ hours
Start altitude:	2575m (8448ft)
High point:	Lamjura La (3530m: 11,581ft)
Height gain:	955m (3133ft)
Descent:	855m (2805ft)
Accommodation:	Lodges at Dagcho, Goyem, Tragdobuk and Junbesi

A fine, but moderately hard day's trekking, this stage leads to a charming village and the valley system known as Solu district on the far side of the Lamjura Danda. At 3530m (11,581ft) the Lamjura La marks the highest point on this trek until you leave Namche Bazaar. In good conditions the crossing should cause no problems, apart from the possibility of headache and breathlessness due to the altitude, but unseasonal snowfall could make this exposed saddle rather unpleasant. On the whole it's a scenically interesting walk, and if you are not bothered by the altitude, it's one to enjoy to the full.

On leaving Sete the route resumes its persistent uphill course, perhaps not with the same degree of severity experienced out of Kenja, but still sufficient to start your lungs heaving. In about an hour you will arrive at **DAGCHO** (2850m: 9350ft, *accommodation, refreshments*), a spartan settlement of tea-houses and lodges built right on the ridge.

Continue straight up the ridge, soon among forests of rhododendrons and pine, and in about 45 minutes or so from Dagcho you should reach the first part of another simple lodge settlement. This is **GOYEM** (3155m: 10,351ft, 2 hours, *accommodation, refreshments*), a two-part village with 5 minutes of trail between them. About a minute after leaving the last building you will come to a trail junction. Ignore the tempting contour path to the right, and instead continue up the ridge, as before, steadily making height in easy windings through thinning forest. Views to the left show far-off snowpeaks again, while behind, Deorali (crossed on the way to Bhandar) is clearly seen. Foothills roll away to a blue distant haze.

Out of forest you come to yet another collection of primitive tea-houses, above which the trail has cut a groove between rhododendrons. In the post-monsoon trekking season the banks here are speckled with the lovely blue gentian *Gentiana depressa*, while rhododendrons come into their own in the spring.

When you reach a mani wall and a nearby stone-built hut on the crest of the ridge, you must leave the ridge and slant left where the path contours through forest. When it forks shortly after, take either option for they rejoin a little later. It's an easy trail now, for the most part fairly level with a few ups and downs, and it emerges from the forest to a large clearing in which there are two simple lodges. From here to the pass will take about 30 minutes.

The trail maintains its contour along the hillside, much of the way having been paved with huge slabs of stone, and then suddenly swings to the right before twisting the last few paces to the **LAMJURA LA** (3530m: 11,581ft, 3-3$^{1}/_{2}$ hours), a wide grassy saddle adorned with a litter of prayer flags, mani walls and great heaps of rock. In clear snow-free conditions without a wind blowing, it's tempting to sit here for a while and enjoy the views. There are no big mountains in sight, but a great swelling of foothills wherever you look, and the valley ahead, into which the descent will go, appears to be utterly charming. As it proves. It is the first of the valleys of Solu district, more properly known to the Sherpas as Shorong.

The descent trail is an obvious one, steep at first as it corkscrews through forest, rough underfoot, too, as it has been cut by teams of packhorses that trade across the pass. There are a few basic tea-houses, both in and out of the forest, but the only village, as such, is Tragdobuk (Taktor) which is situated further down-valley after having wandered through open pastures and between stone-walled fields. **TRAGDOBUK** (2860m: 9383ft, 5 hours, *accommodation, refreshments*) has a primitive-looking lodge at its upper end. In the centre of the village the houses are grouped close together. There's a wind-powered prayer wheel and a small stupa. On reaching this take the trail that slants left ahead - do not take the right-hand trail for this goes to Salleri, way down the valley of the Junbesi Khola.

With about 45 minutes to go before reaching Junbesi the trail makes a gently rising traverse of the left-hand hillside, gaining a little height here, losing a little there. One or two mani walls have been built along the trail; there are also steps in places. Then you come round a bluff and there ahead a high and distant wall of snowpeaks blocks the valley of the Junbesi Khola - Karyolaug, Khatang and Numbur (also known as Shorong Yul Lha - God of the Solu). Below (not far below) lies Junbesi in its own Shangri-La setting; a well laid-out village whose yellow-roofed gompa draws the eye. This first view is appealing and quite idyllic. A choice of trails invite you down.

JUNBESI (2675m: 8776ft) is one of the most delightful of Sherpa villages on this trek. It has a number of comfortable lodges, a shop (not always open), post office, health clinic/hospital, a large school founded by Sir Edmund Hillary in 1964, an interesting monastery, a library next to the post office, a police check-post and a small hydro scheme which provides lighting for the whole village. A number of houses here have their own gardens in which a wide variety of vegetables are grown.

Not only is Junbesi a comfortable village in which to spend a night or two, the valley in which it nestles has much to commend a few days' exploration. From the village itself you cannot see the high peaks that were visible from the trail above, so it could be worth spending time wandering the path that heads north through the upper valley. It is all enticing country, with pinewoods, pastures, small field systems and glacial streams draining out of the arc of

Schoolchildren in Junbesi

mountains at its head. The red panda is thought to exist in some of the high forest areas nearby.

Upvalley, about an hour or so from Junbesi, but on the eastern side of the river, stands the important Thubten Chholing Gompa where a large number of Buddhist monks and nuns study. Visitors are welcome (don't forget to make a donation before leaving).

Beyond Thubten Chholing, above the confluence of the Mampung and Basa Khola rivers, is the village of Phungmuche, site of a Sherpa Arts Centre. This is about 2 hours' walk from Junbesi.

Down-valley, perhaps 3 hours away, are Phaplu and Salleri. Both have trekkers' lodges; Phaplu has a STOL airstrip (scheduled flights to and from Kathmandu) and a hospital built by Hillary's Himalayan Trust, while nearby Salleri (45 minutes from Phaplu) is the headquarters of Solu district. Further south still is Chialsa, where there's a Tibetan camp. From Chialsa a trail climbs to the spectacularly sited Chiwong Gompa, perched on a cliff overlooking Phaplu.

An alternative trail heads north from Phaplu to rejoin the main trail at Ringmo.

JUNBESI - TRAGSINDHO LA - MANIDINGMA (NUNTALA)

Distance:	14 kilometres (9 miles)
Time:	6-7 hours
Start altitude:	2675m (8776ft)
High points:	Everest View (3048m: 10,000ft)
	Tragsindho La (3071m: 10,075ft)
Height gain:	845m (2772ft)
Descent:	1326m (4350ft)
Accommodation:	Lodges at Everest View, Sallung, Ringmo,
	Tragsindho and Manidingma

On this stage Mount Everest is seen for the first time - clouds permitting. Caught among a whole line of impressive mountains it is an exciting view, and one that is very much a tease since it does not last long. Later, as you approach Manidingma, the savage shape of Kusum Kangguru shows itself above the hinted cleft of the Dudh Kosi - the valley that will lead all the way to Everest and which at last is drawing near.

But for most of this stage the big mountains are still remote and unattainable. Instead there are the middle hills to enjoy with their pinewoods, deep valleys and villages, the orchards of Ringmo and another Buddhist gompa at Tragsindho. There are farms and cheese factories, too, along the trail, and one of the most pleasant of all belvedere sections of path between Junbesi and Sallung.

Wander down through Junbesi below the stupa to cross the river by a wooden bridge. A few paces beyond this the path forks. Bear left and rise through a forest of rhododendrons, blue pine and oak on a steady ascent. The trail again divides and once more you take the upper, left-hand option. Soon the forest is left behind and views now overlook the valley which drains towards Phaplu, the steep sides stepped with neat agricultural terraces. Looking back it's possible to see up to the Lamjura La.

The path develops a scenic belvedere course along the hillside, passing one or two farms on the way, and after about 1¹/₂ hours from Junbesi brings you to a lone tea-house. A few minutes later the trail curves round a hillside spur where a group of buildings, consisting of lodge, shop and cheese factory, hug the bend. This is **EVEREST VIEW** (3048m: 10,000ft, 1¹/₂ hours, *accommodation, refreshments*). And what a view! If you're lucky a magnificent line of high, dramatic snowpeaks will draw your attention towards the north-east. Mount Everest marks the left-hand end of this line, but seems dwarfed by some of the others. Also in view are Thamserku, Lhotse, Nuptse, Kusum Kangguru, Kangtega, Mera Peak and Makalu. It is a view to savour.

The near-level, beaten-earth trail continues, now with those mountains ahead seen across a succession of intervening ridges, one of which will be crossed later at the Tragsindho La. The path follows an even contour before sloping down to the attractive village of **SALLUNG** (2953m: 9688ft, 2 hours, *accommodation, refreshments*) where views remain as magnificent as before. There are several lodges here, with gardens full of produce.

After leaving Sallung the route begins the long twisting descent to the Beni Khola (also known as the Dudh Kund or Ringmo Khola) with Ringmo seen on the opposite flank and the white stupa marking the Tragsindho La well above it. Although views of Everest and its neighbours are soon lost, at certain points on the trail it's possible to see the fine shape of Karyolaug (6681m: 21,920ft) off to the left.

The Beni Khola is crossed on a suspension bridge at 2599m (8527ft), and from it a short, but fairly steep climb heads up to a trail junction (the right-hand path is that which leads to Phaplu) and the lodges of **RINGMO** (2805m: 9203ft, 3¹/₂-4 hours, *accommodation, refreshments*). Orchards of apple, apricot and peach line the path that takes you past the lodges and up towards the main part of the village.

As you wander up the stone path to the village proper, you pass two mani walls, the second of which is nearly 50m long. Immediately on reaching the far end of this it is important to leave the main trail and head off to the right. The junction is not very clear, but the path improves within a few paces.

Now the way leads up among trees and soon comes to a T junction of trails. Go sharp left here (the right-hand trail goes to another cheese factory and lodge in about 10 minutes), and soon cross a clearing with a simple tea-house in it. The trail climbs on and is badly eroded. In less than an hour from Ringmo you come to the **TRAGSINDHO LA** (3071m: 10,075ft, 4¹/₂-5 hours, *refreshments*), an untidy pass marked by a large white stupa, tea-house and a flotilla of prayer flags. It's the last ridge-crossing on the eastbound trek leading to the Dudh Kosi, and the point where you pass from Solu district to the region known as Pharak, which links the Sherpa country of Solu with that of Khumbu.

The descent on the eastern side of the pass to Tragsindho Gompa is short but steep. **TRAGSINDHO** (2611m: 8566ft, 5 hours 15 minutes *accommodation, refreshments*) is an assorted cluster of buildings, mostly serving the large and impressive-looking monastery nearby. There is also a lodge here and a small shop. If clouds allow, there's a superb view of Kusum Kangguru to the north-east.

Below the shop the trail swings left and then forks. Bear right to follow round the gompa's lower boundary fence, passing one or two houses. Eventually the path becomes more obvious as it descends in a long sweep round the hillside. Part of the route goes through forest, part through agricultural land. The village of Manidingma is seen long before you reach it, and there's a lodge standing alone beside the trail a few minutes before entering. Attractive from afar, the reality of Manidingma unfortunately does not match one's first impressions.

MANIDINGMA (2194m: 7198ft) is also known as Nuntala, a village of lodges and shops facing one another across a broad, paved main street. It is a rather untidy place, forming a direct contrast to Junbesi.

MANIDINGMA - DUDH KOSI - KHARIKHOLA

Distance:	8 kilometres (5 miles)
Time:	4 hours
Start altitude:	2194m (7198ft)
Low point:	Dudh Kosi (1493m: 4898ft)
Descent:	701m (2300ft)
High point:	Kharikhola (2072m: 6798ft)
Height gain:	579m (1900ft)
Accommodation:	Lodges at Jubing and Kharikhola

Although this is only a short stage it's an extremely pleasant one, with good mountain views at times and some outstanding fertile countryside to pass through. It's also a significant stage, for at last the eastbound journey across

the middle hills reaches the valley of the Dudh Kosi, from where the route
begins to head northward, following the river which drains all the Khumbu
region of high mountains. Although this is Sherpa country, the first village
on the trail up the Dudh Kosi is not inhabited by Sherpas, but by Rai hill folk.
Rai villages are found throughout eastern Nepal, but Solu-Khumbu is about
as far west as they've settled, and Jubing is the only non-Sherpa village on
the Everest trek after Sete. Rai houses and bridges are often decorated with
garlands of marigolds.

The day's trek may be divided into two equal parts. The first involves
descent to the Dudh Kosi, the second entails a steady climb to Kharikhola, a
strung-out village with some fine lodges. From Manidingma to Kharikhola
is a traditional porter-stage, but independent trekkers could continue as far
as Bupsa, another hour or so further on, thereby shortening the next fairly
long stage to Chaumrikharka.

Morning views from Manidingma are often much clearer than would no
doubt have been experienced on arrival, so as you leave the village look
northward where Karyolaug may be seen, and north-east to Kusum Kangguru.
The latter peak will be in view for much of the descent to the Dudh Kosi. The
trail leading down to the river is clear and obvious, but it has some steep
sections and after rain or a heavy dew may be quite slippery.

About 15 minutes from Manidingma the trail forks; both path options
rejoin soon after. It's a delightful descent, the path winding round the
steep plunging hillside that has been immaculately terraced - hundreds
of narrow shelves stepping one after another down to the thin ribbon
of silver seen far below where the Deku Khola drains the hills. It's a
glorious landscape, growing more and more lush as you draw nearer
to the river. Numerous houses dot the hillside, but there are few
lodges or tea-houses on the trail, and you will have been walking for
almost an hour before you come to Hotel Quiet View, which at one
time bore an incongruous sign claiming it to be just 5 minutes from
Nuntala (Manidingma)!

It takes about 1¹/₂ hours to reach the confluence of the Deku Khola
and Dudh Kosi rivers. Just before coming to the suspension bridge
strung across the Dudh Kosi you pass a complex of tea-houses
overlooking the river. After this the next opportunity for refreshment
is at Jubing, a little over half an hour's uphill walk away.

Cross the suspension bridge to the east bank of the Dudh Kosi

(Milk River), and wander along the trail that swings to the left, then rises up the hillside to **JUBING** (1676m: 5499ft, 2 hours 15 minutes, *accommodation, refreshments*). This is a lovely village set among fertile terraces; a bright and colourful place, clean and tidy and with flowers and vegetables growing beside the trail late into the autumn. Streams run through the village, one of which powers a small mill. There are several lodges; one or two appear especially inviting.

Passing through Jubing, in 20 minutes the trail makes a sharp right-hand bend, with another path cutting from it and heading among the terraces. Do not be tempted by this alternative, but keep on the main trail to climb up to a group of three buildings standing about 10 minutes' walk away. On reaching these (*refreshments available*) the trail again divides. One climbs directly up the hillside above the buildings and crosses a small pass before dropping to Kharikhola. The other, which is recommended, continues past the buildings to slant across the hillside, affording good views over massed terraces. After reaching a high point the trail rounds a corner, then looks across to the village of Kharikhola scattered over the hillside ahead, on different levels of terracing.

The way descends, then undulates a little, before entering **KHARIKHOLA** (2072m: 6798ft). All the lodges here are set beside the main trail, as are several shops and tea-houses. It's a clean and pleasant village with friendly local people and some comfortable accommodation. After Junbesi Kharikhola is one of the nicest places to stay in, and its shops supply an amazing variety of goods. The village has a thriving school. It also has its own electricity supply.
Note: Since the next stage to Chaumrikharka is rather long (about 8 hours) tea-house trekkers might consider it worth continuing beyond Kharikhola as far as Bupsa, seen on the ridge ahead, about 1-1¹/₂ hours' walk away. Failing this, make a point of starting early out of Kharikhola in the morning.

KHARIKHOLA - PUIYAN - CHAUMRIKHARKA

Distance:	14 kilometres (9 miles)
Time:	8 hours
Start altitude:	2072m (6798ft)
High point:	Khari La (2850m: 9350ft)
Height gain:	1191m (3907ft)
Descent:	550m (1804ft)
Accommodation:	Lodges at Bupsa, Puiyan, Surkhe and Chaumrikharka (and Lukla)

This is quite a demanding walk, much of it in forest and with a fair amount of height gain and loss; a hiccup of a trail where views are largely constrained by trees. Yet despite the absence of views it will be evident that progress is being made towards Khumbu, and by the time you reach Chaumrikharka you'll know the big mountains are not far ahead. On this stage there are some long stretches between tea-houses, so plenty of liquids should be carried, especially during hot weather.

Out of Kharikhola the trail descends a little, crosses a sturdy suspension bridge, then begins a steep, heart-pounding climb to Bupsa. The way is clear, yet uncompromising, but there's a tea-house providing an excuse to rest before making the final climb up and across a landslip area. **BUPSA** (2350m: 7710ft, 1 hour 15 minutes, *accommodation, refreshments*) is perched at the head of a precarious slope. It has a clutch of lodges and tea-houses, and a small gompa.

Beyond the village the trek enters a jungly phase, the trail rising through damp forest with streams and small waterfalls cascading. There are a few simple tea-houses, but nothing more substantial until you reach Puiyan. Continuing to gain height, about 2 hours from Bupsa you should come to a high point at about 2850m (9350ft). This is below the unseen Khari La, a pass crossed on the original route from Kharikhola, but the present trail, created in the early 1980s, saves both time and effort by avoiding it.

This high point is not a true pass, but the turning of a spur of hillside marked by a mani wall and prayer flags. From it you may be able to see the mountain which rises above Namche, Khumbui Yul Lha (Khumbila). The Dudh Kosi has bored its way through the gorge-like valley hundreds of metres below the hillside here, and in places you gain a sensational view into the depths of the gorge.

There is still a little more height to gain, and a return to forest where the way resumes its switchback course, cutting into the deep glen of the Puiyan Khola. Across the stream you soon come to **PUIYAN** (2796m: 9173ft, 4-4¹/₂ hours, *accommodation, refreshments*). This is not really a village, but a few basic lodges and tea-houses set in the forest.

After leaving Puiyan there is much less forest to wander through and the trail enjoys a more open aspect. It continues as a switchback, and steadily increases altitude until the Dudh Kosi itself rushes a thousand metres or more below. In places the route is quite exposed. About an hour from Puiyan you come to another high point on a spur with prayer flags strung above the path. Here you have a splendid view up the Dudh Kosi's valley, and also overlooking Lukla and its airstrip. Far below the few buildings of Surkhe may be seen.

The path winds through forest once more, then makes a long and seemingly endless descent on a flight of rough stone steps to reach **SURKHE** (2300m: 7546ft, 6-6¹/₂ hours, *accommodation, refreshments*). A few buildings stand amid farmland in a basin just below the trail, and two or three lodges line the path itself. A stream runs through the basin.

After crossing the stream you begin to climb yet again, and about 15 minutes later come to a mani wall where the trail forks. The right-hand option leads to Lukla; the continuing trail is the main path to Chaumrikharka.

Main Trail to Chaumrikharka:

The trail climbs on beyond the mani wall and crosses another stream which drains down from Lukla. Then there's a splendid waterfall pouring through a deep gorge. The way finally heads up among some boulders, goes alongside mani walls and reaches the first part of **CHAUMRIKHARKA** (2591m: 8501ft), an amalgamation of villages where there are several lodges.

Route to Lukla:

At the trail junction by the mani wall bear right and go up some steps. These lead to a clear path that climbs steeply, goes through rhododendron forest, then makes a contour to the left. Eventually come to a rough pastureland basin in which there are a couple of buildings. Cross a bridge on the left, then climb in loops up the hillside to reach another building at the entrance to a fairly level stretch of farmland. There's an insignificant-looking trail junction at this point. Find a narrow path climbing steeply to the right among shrubbery. It soon joins a more substantial trail that leads directly to **LUKLA** (2860m: 9383ft), about 1 hour 15 minutes from the mani wall junction.

LUKLA

LUKLA (2860m: 9383ft) has developed into a thriving township of lodges, restaurants and shops in response to all the business brought to it by construction of the airstrip in 1965. Daily, when the weather permits, plane-loads of trekkers and mountaineers fly in, and out of, this rather unattractive hilltop perch. But when the weather does not permit - ah, then Lukla has an atmosphere all its own!

When clouds hang low for several days at a time, which is not at all uncommon, literally hundreds of people crowd the lodges in a mass of seething frustration. Never mind recent days of calm splendour, of patient hours spent gazing at the mountains, of learning the art of contentment. Suddenly you're plunged back into the world of third-party schedules and that's when the blood pressure rises. In spells of bad weather Lukla is a hot-bed of rumour. There's a plane on the way. There won't be any flights for three days. You've lost your place on the waiting list. There is no waiting list!

Should you be booked on the first flight out on Monday (or any other) morning, and the plane does not arrive, you'd imagine that you would be automatically placed on the next flight to go. But that's not the way it works at Lukla. Your name goes to the bottom of the list, and only when all other scheduled passengers have flown will you find a seat on a plane out. It follows, then, that when a backlog builds up due to persistent bad weather, the illogicality of this system creates a frenzy of despair.

What can you do about it? Well, if you don't have 2 or 3 days to walk out to Phaplu (and try to catch one of the 3-a-week flights from there) or about 5 days' walking to reach Jiri for a day's bus ride back to Kathmandu, you'd better breathe deeply, think over the delights of the past few days' trekking, and become philosophical about it all. In a month's time the horrors of Lukla will just be part of life's rich pattern of experience, and if you have friends who've never been there, maybe you can at least dine out on the story - which won't need much elaboration.

Difficulties have been slightly eased by Nepal Air running flights to and from Lukla, as well as those of RNAC. Helicopters are also used on occasion, to help relieve a backlog, but seats are very expensive.

But the Lukla experience is not always a painful one, and if you've been walking in from Jiri you may decide that you'd rather fly out, if possible, than walk all the way back to the roadhead. So you didn't buy a ticket in advance in Kathmandu? Don't worry, there's still a chance to get one organised.

Book in for a night at the Himalaya Lodge (situated immediately above the runway) and speak to Dawa Tshiring Sherpa who owns it. He is Lukla's Mr Fixit, and although not an official of either Royal Nepal or Nepal Air, if it's at all possible to get you booked on a flight out, he will. Tickets must be paid for in US dollars - as in Kathmandu. Dawa also provides flight information and ticket reconfirmation. He can arrange guides and porters for your trek too. (It may be that others in Lukla can provide a similar service, but I have no personal experience of them.)

Having arrived in Lukla, either on foot from Jiri, or by plane from Kathmandu, you'll be anxious to leave and head upvalley towards Namche Bazaar and the mountains of Khumbu. Apart from the initial easy downhill walk to Choplung, the route is the same as that taken by trekkers coming from Chaumrikharka, details of which follow.

As it takes time to get porter- or yak-loads organised, group trekkers will probably have a short day's walk ending at Phakding or, at the most, Mondzo on the edge of the Sagarmatha National Park. Independent trekkers may be tempted to push on further towards Namche. But if you've just flown in to Lukla this would be unwise. Namche is an easy day and a half's walk away, but the advanced altitude is enough to cause problems for anyone who rushes it. Prepare yourself for a steady walk and you'll enjoy the rest of your trek in Khumbu. Don't spoil it with impatience that could so easily lead to mountain sickness.

LUKLA - CHOPLUNG

Distance:	3 kilometres (2 miles)
Time:	30 minutes - 1 hour
Start altitude:	2860m (9383ft)
Descent:	200m (656ft)

As recommended above, do not set yourself a goal that's too ambitious for a first day, but instead be content to call a halt at either Phakding, or one of the other overnight options between there and Mondzo. Times given for the route beyond Choplung apply to the route from Chaumrikharka, so you should add another 30 minutes to them.

From Lukla the Namche trail is broad, clear and obvious. It heads north away from the airstrip and along a lodge-lined street, then slopes downhill, soon to reach a low region of agricultural land which it skirts along the right-hand edge. In little more than half an hour from Lukla you'll come to a junction of trails in the neat lodge village of **CHOPLUNG** (2660m: 8727ft, *accommodation, refreshments*). Bear right here on the main trail to Namche.

The remainder of the route is described below.

CHAUMRIKHARKA - PHAKDING - MONDZO

Distance:	10 kilometres (6¹/₂ miles)
Time:	4-4¹/₂ hours
Start altitude:	2591m (8501ft)
High point:	Benkar (2905m: 9531ft)
Height gain:	410m (1345ft)
Descent:	314m (1030ft)
Accommodation:	Lodges in Choplung, Phakding, Benkar, Chumoa and Mondzo

Half an hour after leaving Chaumrikharka the nature of the Everest trek changes, for it is at Choplung that the trail from Lukla joins yours. Suddenly there will be many more people to share the way; not only those who have just arrived by air from Kathmandu, but others on their way out - trekkers, mountaineers and their Sherpas and porters or strings of yaks. Below Choplung you probably saw no yaks at all, but now no stage will be complete without finding yourself forced to give way on the trail to these lumbering, shaggy beasts with menacing horns and, often, a pack or two strapped upon their backs. When faced by a yak on a mountain trail always let it pass on the downhill side.

On this stage the scenery also changes in a dramatic way. Now the walling mountains wear snow and ice. Vegetation is less luxurious and the valley takes on a savage appearance.

Out of Chaumrikharka the trail passes through fields and in half an hour comes to **CHOPLUNG** (2660m: 8727ft, *accommodation, refreshments*), a neat village with several lodges, a shop or two and the junction with the path to Lukla. The way continues easily, without any severe uphill stretches for a while, but then drops suddenly to the Kusum Khola in the mouth of a narrow gorge, through which may be spied the graceful summit of Kusum Kangguru (6369m: 20,896ft), an impressive but difficult 'trekking peak'. Across the bridge here you pass a simple lodge and then climb a stone stairway, turn a corner and soon begin to slope down again to the village of **GHAT** (2591m: 8501ft, *accommodation, refreshments*). It's a strung-out village with several lodges and tea-houses. At its upper end you pass two large prayer wheels, and immediately beyond these, some huge boulders that have been brightly decorated with the Buddhist mantra: *Om Mani Padme Hum.*

Now the way heads through a rough, rock-strewn area, but it soon improves and with a small amount of up and down brings you to the larger settlement of **PHAKDING** (2652m: 8701ft, 2 hours, *accommodation, refreshments*). The village is in two parts, separated by about 10 minutes' worth of trail and a suspension bridge over the Dudh Kosi. Both sections have lodges, but groups often choose to camp on the west bank of the river in flat meadows directly in front of two of the lodges. Phakding is used as a first night's stop by groups who arrived in Lukla by one of the later flights from Kathmandu.

Cross the long suspension bridge over the river, and after passing between two lodges the path curves to the right, rises along the hillside and soon crosses a tributary glen. There are a few very simple lodges, tea-houses and solitary farmsteads along the west bank of the

On the main trail from Lukla to Namche a huge boulder is adorned with the mantra Om Mani Padme Hum, *While prayer flags hang from lofty poles*

Dudh Kosi, and about 30 minutes from Phakding you come to the single lodge and camp ground of **TOKTOK**. Not long after this you pass **BENKAR** (2905m: 9531ft, 3 hours, *accommodation, refreshments*) which also has lodging.

The trail descends to the river and crosses to the east bank again on a wooden cantilever bridge, then a few minutes later reaches **CHUMOA** (3½ hours, *accommodation, refreshments*) where there are more lodges set among graceful conifers and rhododendrons. The way descends steeply to cross another tributary stream, the Kyashar Khola, which drains a glacial system between Kusum Kangguru and Thamserku, then climbs again and shortly after enters Mondzo, on the edge of Sagarmatha National Park.

MONDZO (2835m: 9301ft) is a small village of shingle-roofed houses and a few lodges. There's a gompa nearby. From here to Namche Bazaar involves a walk of only half a day.

MONDZO - NAMCHE BAZAAR

Distance:	5 kilometres (3 miles)
Time:	3-3¹/₂ hours
Start altitude:	2835m (9301ft)
High point:	Namche Bazaar 3446m (11,306ft)
Height gain:	611m (2005ft)
Accommodation:	Lodges at Namche Bazaar

From Mondzo the trail to Namche leads through the narrow cleft of the Dudh Kosi gorge, a stark defile whose bed has been ravaged several times by natural calamities. One of these occurred in 1977 when a landslip on the lower slopes of Ama Dablam blocked a stream. When the lake that had built up behind it burst its banks, a wall of water rushed down through the valley, tearing away bridges, as well as part of the village of Jorsale, killing three people. A similar catastrophe happened in 1985 when a glacial lake above Thame also broke free, destroyed a 2 million dollar dam and wrought havoc all the way down

The lodges at Mondzo crowd the trail on the edge of the Sagarmatha National Park

the Bhote Kosi and Dudh Kosi valleys. The route through the gorge may not be exactly as described, since it is subject to frequent change as nature has her way.

Minutes after leaving Mondzo you come to the entrance of the Sagarmatha National Park. At the large building here trekking permits and National Park entry permits are checked. Note that if you're carrying a video camera you'll have to pay to take it into the Park. At present this costs US \$100. A brief summary of Park rules is printed on the reverse of the entry permit. No firewood is allowed to be cut from forests within the National Park boundaries, and as a consequence it will be necessary for campers to carry kerosene stoves and sufficient fuel to last throughout their trek. Kerosene is sold in Lukla and Namche.

Once through the gate the trail descends to river level and into the small village of **THAOG**. Pass two or three houses, then turn left in the middle of the village between some buildings and cross the Dudh Kosi on a long suspension bridge. The trail resumes on the west bank for a while, passes a few tea-houses and simple lodges in **JORSALE** (2775m: 9104ft, *accommodation, refreshments*) then returns to the east bank by a smaller bridge.

Now the way heads along the stony bed of the valley, winding among rocks towards the point where the Bhote Kosi and Dudh Kosi come together below a mountain wall upon which unseen Namche Bazaar is perched. The Bhote Kosi enters through a gorge on the left, the Dudh Kosi from a gorge on the right. To reach Namche involves crossing the Dudh Kosi gorge on a high suspension bridge slung way above the river not far upstream of its confluence with the Bhote Kosi. The path leaves the valley bed and climbs steeply with the aid of some steps to gain the bridge.

Across the bridge it descends a few metres, then begins the last uphill to Namche, a climb that will take about 1¹/₂-2 hours. Steep in places, the broad trail snakes its way up the slope. About halfway up there's a tea-house with a brief view of Everest, Nuptse and Lhotse seen from the ridge behind it. Continuing, mostly among trees, you eventually come to a group of buildings, soon after which the trail forks. Take the right-hand path. It climbs steeply, turns a corner and brings you directly into one of the lower streets of Namche Bazaar.

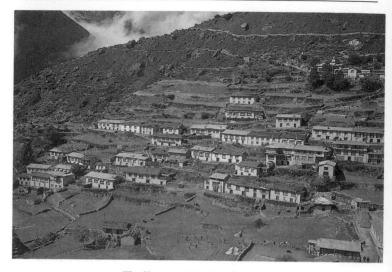

The Sherpa capital, Namche Bazaar

NAMCHE BAZAAR (3446m: 11,306ft) is the Sherpa 'capital' and administrative centre for Khumbu district. The headquarters of the Sagarmatha National Park and a military post are both situated above the town, just off the trail to Thyangboche. Namche has its own electricity supply powered by a low-key hydro scheme financed by UNESCO. The town has a great many lodges, restaurants and camping grounds. It has a post office, bank, police check-post and a dental clinic. Numerous shops line its narrow streets and sell a vast range of goods, including postcards, films, medical supplies, food, clothing, paperbacks, souvenirs and all sorts of second-hand expedition equipment. Boots, down jackets and sleeping bags can be rented here.

Saturday is market day. Then the place is crowded with porters and traders, some of whom have come over the Nangpa La from Tibet, others having walked for several days from the Nepalese foothills carrying *dokos* of fruit or vegetables that are impossible to grow in Khumbu. It's a bright, bustling affair that is often over by midday, followed by Sherpas celebrating with friends from afar in a local chang house.

For most trekkers, especially those walking in from Jiri, Namche has a special appeal. To gain the town is almost a goal in itself. Yet Bill Tilman, one of the first Westerners ever to arrive here, was peculiarly dismissive: 'Namche Bazar' he wrote, 'has never ranked as a "forbidden city". It is far from being a city, and it has remained unvisited not because of any very serious difficulties in the way, but because no one has thought it worth the trouble of overcoming them'. 'Nevertheless' he confessed, 'it had for long been my humble Mecca'. Many a trekker would echo those last words.

A biennial Everest Marathon, held in late-November (odd-numbered years) finishes in Namche. After allowing sufficient time to acclimatise, competitors race the 42 kilometres (26 miles) from Gorak Shep down through the Khumbu valley via Pangboche and Thyangboche to Namche Bazaar, the winners finishing in around 4 hours. On your return from Gorak Shep or Lobuche, that sort of timing will either inspire or appal you, depending on your point of view. With the large number of athletes and supporters who attend this event, the trail and the lodges alongside it can become overcrowded during the few days leading up to, and following, the race.

As you stand amid the shallow hillside horseshoe that curves round Namche, gazing across to the huge wall of Kwangde that soars out of the Bhote Kosi valley west of town, there's an understandable sense of relief that you've made it this far, and a buzz of anticipation for great things in store just over the hill.

Because of the altitude it will be necessary to spend at the very minimum two nights here to aid acclimatisation. That does not mean you have to sit around all day in a lodge or restaurant, although it may be tempting to do so. There are some interesting walks that will help the acclimatisation process, and at the same time provide a scenic introduction to the high country of Khumbu. The following section outlines some of these walks.

TIME IN NAMCHE

The following very pleasant 3¹/₂-4 hour circuit, visiting two traditional Sherpa villages and providing stunning views, reaches a high point of about 3870m (12,697ft) at the Japanese-built **EVEREST VIEW HOTEL**, where you can have lunch on the balcony with one of the world's great mountain panoramas spread before you. This is a fine way to aid acclimatisation.

Take the main Thyangboche trail which leaves Namche's bowl over its eastern rim, a broad, well trodden path that soon provides a heart-stopping view of Everest, Nuptse, Lhotse and Ama Dablam walling the Khumbu valley. In mid-distance it may be possible to see the Thyangboche monastery jutting above a wooded ridge.

Continue along the trail for about 1¹/₄ hours to reach the settlement of **KYANGJUMA** (3600m: 11,811ft, *accommodation, refreshments*). Soon after entering this little hamlet look for a narrow path that climbs to the left, skirting a number of walled fields. It winds through a lovely scoop of hillside brightened with flame-coloured berberis in the autumn and pocked with rocks. There are magnificent views back to Ama Dablam.

The faint path reaches more drystone walls leading directly to **KHUMJUNG** (3780m: 12,402ft, *accommodation, refreshments*), a large stony Sherpa village that appears remarkably unspoilt in its hidden valley. Note the water supply and large chorten at the entrance to the village. To the left of this a trail heads up a ridge, initially by way of a series of stone steps, and is the route to Everest View Hotel. Before heading up that trail, however, it would be worth exploring Khumjung and the neighbouring village of **KHUNDE** (3841m: 12,602ft) where there's a small hospital - another product of Hillary's Himalayan Trust, as is Khumjung's high school. Allow at least 1¹/₂ hours to explore both these villages. The sacred mountain of the Khumbu, Khumbui Yul Lha, or Khumbila for short, rises behind Khumjung, and is seen from almost every part of the Khumbu district.

The trail that links the Khumjung water supply and the Japanese hotel is a delight. The ridge it climbs is clothed with rhododendrons and stands of pine, and views are consistently dramatic. It leads directly to the 12-room **EVEREST VIEW HOTEL**, but you don't see the building until the very last moment as it has been cleverly

Ama Dablam, considered to be one of the most beautiful mountains in the world

designed to blend into the hilltop. Typically Japanese in appearance, the main entrance is by a long and elegant flight of steps that approach among shrubs and trees. The surrounding pines seem almost to have been positioned in order to frame views of Thamserku, Kangtega and Ama Dablam.

Whilst both design and situation are remarkable, the practicalities of building such a hotel on this ridgetop are questionable. All the hotel's water has to be carried up from Khumjung. It's very expensive to stay here, and the clientele are invariably flown in from Kathmandu to the airstrip at Syangboche above Namche, at an altitude of about 3720m (12,205ft), which is dangerously high for anyone not acclimatised. As a result guests frequently need bottled oxygen, or use a pressurised room just to survive the experience. The hotel is often almost completely empty. But it's a great place to visit for lunch.

Leave the hotel by its main entrance and follow the path leading from it. It reaches a lodge and then forks. Both options lead to Namche, while another goes ahead beside the lodge, then through shrubbery to descend to the end of Syangboche's airstrip. From there you can see Namche steeply below. A variety of trails lead down to it.

95

More direct trails than the one via Kyangjuma lead to both **KHUNDE** and **KHUMJUNG** from Namche. One climbs a much braided steep route from a large rock near the top, eastern end of town, approached by way of the Thyangboche trail mentioned above, and leads to Syangboche airstrip. This is the trail used on descent from the Everest View Hotel. Walk along the airstrip, then find a continuing trail that climbs north-east past a large chorten, through pinewoods and into a glen where Khumjung high school is situated. Bear left for Khunde, right for the trail to Everest View Hotel.

Another route from Namche to Khunde leaves town from the street junction just west of the bank. This also climbs to Syangboche, continues to gain height in order to cross a wooded ridge to Khunde. Allow about $1^1/2$ hours from Namche.

Yet another acclimatisation walk visits **THAME** in the valley of the Bhote Kosi to the west of Namche. As it is 350m (1148ft) higher than Namche, and takes about 3 hours to reach, it might be worth spending at least one night there before returning to Namche and heading on towards Everest. The Bhote Kosi is a very fine valley, but because it is headed by the Nangpa La which leads into Tibet, it's out of bounds to foreigners beyond Thame. Thame itself is a pleasant village with glorious views of Thamserku amd Kangtega. It was the birthplace of Tenzing Norgay who first climbed Everest with Ed Hillary in 1953, and is the site of an important Buddhist gompa where the Mani Rimdu festival is celebrated during the May full moon.

The trail to Thame leaves Namche Bazaar by way of the town's gompa on the western side of the horseshoe basin, crosses the rim and goes through forest before reaching **PHURTE**, where there's a forest nursery. Crossing a tributary which drains the Kyajo glacier, the route continues to **THAMO**, **THOMDE** and finally **THAME** (*accommodation, refreshments*). The gompa is found to the west of the village. The route to Rolwaling, crossing the Trashi Labtsa pass, heads up the valley behind Thame.

Cholatse, Taboche and the Ngozumpa glacier, from Gokyo Ri
Mount Everest from the north *(Photo: Roland Hiss)*

Summit cairn on Kala Pattar and the head of the Khumbu valley
Pumori (Mallory's 'Daughter Peak') seen from Kala Pattar

NAMCHE BAZAAR TO LOBUCHE, GORAK SHEP AND KALA PATTAR

Beyond Namche the trail inevitably leads towards the heart of the highest mountain landscape on earth; a dramatic scene of ice-chiselled peaks and glacier-scoured valleys. In Khumbu valleys villages have a stark and solemn kind of beauty. They look out over an uncompromising land where agriculture is at its most basic, where husbandry of the soil appears at first to have progressed no further than the 16th century when the first Sherpas came over the mountains from Tibet. The humble potato, staple of their diet, was brought here in the 1830s, and its introduction is reckoned to have been one of the most significant events in Sherpa history until, that is, Khumbu was opened to Western influence in the 1950s.

Before the trekking invasion Pangboche was the highest permanently settled village in the valley. But now both Dingboche, formerly a summer-only community at 4343m (14,249ft), and Pheriche (4252m: 13,950ft), until recently a temporary yak-herder's settlement, have year-round occupation, and lodge-owners keep the yak-dung fires burning as high as Lobuche (4930m: 16,175ft) and Gorak Shep (5184m: 17,008ft) late into the post-monsoon trekking season.

Trekking beyond Namche is quite a different experience to that of trekking from Jiri to Namche. In some ways it is less strenuous, for there are fewer corrugations to tackle; there are no trails crossing the grain of land that have to be followed - although options exist. But here the altitude plays a dominant part. Now above 3000m (10,000ft) it is important to recognise the need to gain height gradually in order to allow the body to adapt to the thinning air, and you are recommended to spend two nights in either Pheriche or Dingboche to aid that process before continuing to Lobuche or Gorak Shep. It is important to drink plenty of liquids, even if you don't feel particularly thirsty, as the body can easily become dehydrated at altitude. Be aware, too, of other signs of mountain sickness, and read again the section on this under Health Matters in the Introduction.

The mountain scenery of Khumbu, of course, is about as dramatic as anyone could wish. Every step of the way, visibility permitting,

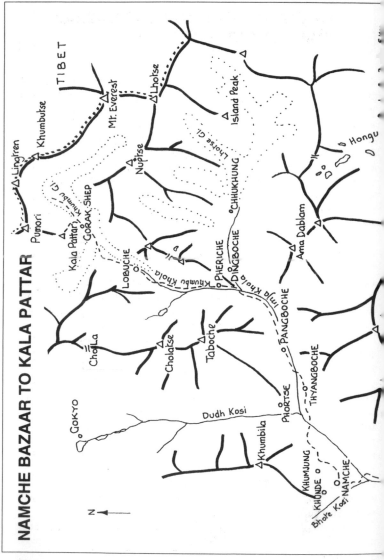

NAMCHE BAZAAR TO KALA PATTAR

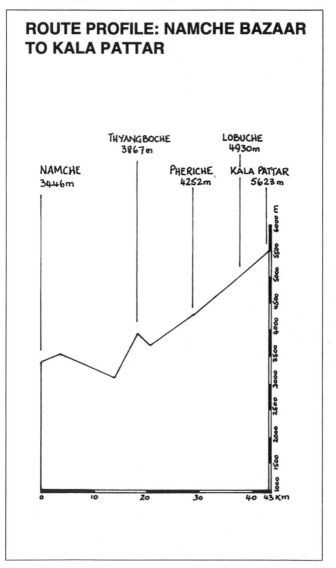

ROUTE PROFILE: NAMCHE BAZAAR TO KALA PATTAR

NAMCHE
3446m

THYANGBOCHE
3867m

PHERICHE
4252m

LOBUCHE
4930m

KALA PATTAR
5623m

will be accompanied by huge, soaring peaks, their summit snows either dazzling in the sunshine or teasing through a drift of wayward cloud.

As before, there is no shortage of accommodation along the trail, and new lodges are being added to the route annually. Some of these are very fine, but as you progress towards the head of the high valley systems, so they become understandably less sophisticated and more expensive to stock with food. Prices rise, standards fall, but the mountain experience grows more profound. Khumbu is probably the coldest trekking region in Nepal, with night-time temperatures demanding use of good-quality, four-season sleeping bags whether you're camping or sleeping in a lodge. Stay warm, stay healthy, and absorb all this fabulous region has to offer.

NAMCHE BAZAAR - THYANGBOCHE

Distance:	19 kilometres (12 miles)
Time:	4-4½ hours
Start altitude:	3446m (11,306ft)
Low point:	Dudh Kosi (3247m: 10,653ft)
Descent:	350m (1148ft)
High point:	Thyangboche (3867m: 12,687ft)
Height gain:	771m (2530ft)
Accommodation:	Lodges at Kyangjuma, Sanasa, Trashingo, Phunki Tenga and Thyangboche

Thyangboche, or Tengboche, is one of those magical places of which dreams are made. Its situation, on a wooded ridge above acres of rhododendron forest, is truly idyllic. Thamserku and Kangtega wall it to the south. Graceful Ama Dablam holds one's attention nearby, while the vast Nuptse-Lhotse wall blocks the valley ahead, with the crown of Mount Everest peering above it.

Many trekkers go no farther than the meadows of Thyangboche, or if they do, it's a there-and-back walk to Pangboche. That will still be a rewarding trek, but anyone with sufficient time, energy and enthusiasm will be drawn as close to Everest as possible. Without question the quality of scenery experienced from Thyangboche is of the highest. Beyond there it will not be better - just different. Very different.

This stage serves as the best possible introduction to Khumbu. The trail is exposed in places, and as it makes a high belvedere way above the river, so the drama grows. It's a busy trail with much coming and going. There will undoubtedly be caravans of laden yaks lumbering along the path, and in dry conditions their hooves scuff the dust into small clouds. Again the warning is given to make sure you are uphill as they pass, for an inadvertent nudge from a horn, flank or load, could so easily result in your being sent crashing down the hillside to the river. End of trek. End of trekker.

The Thyangboche trail climbs out of Namche's bowl up the eastern hillside, passing the police check-post. For your own safety don't forget to show your trekking permit and enter details in the book. The upper part of Namche, where the National Park headquarters and army post are situated, is known as Chorkang. The trail crosses the Namche rim at this point, then makes a fine, easy contour along the hillside with Thamserku and Kangtega gazing down as you approach a left-hand bend where suddenly you're stopped in your tracks by a stunning view of Everest, Nuptse, Lhotse and Ama Dablam, and with Thyangboche's monastery seen as a speck on the crest of a dark ridge in mid-distance.

Now the trail makes a modest switchback along the steeply plunging hillside, and in a little over an hour from Namche comes to a single tea-house set behind a low wall. This enjoys one of the great views of the area, and it's very pleasant to sit at the table outside and relax with a pot of sweet lemon tea before you and huge mountains all around. A few minutes after this you come to **KYANGJUMA** (3600m: 11,811ft, 1¼ hours, *accommodation, refreshments*), a collection of lodges that gaze out at Ama Dablam.

From here the trail goes through a thinly wooded area and brings you to **SANASA** (3580m: 11,745ft, 1 hour 20 minutes, *accommodation, refreshments*) with a few more lodges. Both here and in Kyangjuma souvenirs, claimed to be from Tibet, are laid out beside the trail. If you're interested in buying, it's better to wait until your return rather than add any more weight to the rucksack.

Continue along the clear path that makes a long sloping curve round the hillside before descending to the large village of **TRASHINGO** where there's a lodge and tea-house. Most of the village stands back from the trail, but just below it you pass a tree nursery financed by the Himalayan Trust. The way then begins a steepish descent through forest to the Dudh Kosi. Just before reaching the suspension bridge that crosses the river you will pass one more tea-house.

At 3247m (10,653ft) this is the lowest point on the trek since the approach to Namche Bazaar. A short distance upstream the Imja Khola and Dudh Kosi rivers converge. The main valley becomes that of the Imja Khola, while the Dudh Kosi's headwaters drain the glaciers of Gokyo's valley north-west of Thyangboche. From the bridge over the Dudh Kosi there's a long, steady 2-hour climb to Thyangboche, another 620m (2034ft) up the hill ahead. Don't rush it, but get into a steady rhythm and enjoy the walk, keeping alert for signs of musk deer and Himalayan tahr (a form of wild goat) in the woods as you go.

Just beyond the suspension bridge you enter the village of **PHUNKI TENGA** (3250m: 10,663ft, 2 hours, *accommodation, refreshments*) where a series of water-driven prayer wheels lines the trail. Now the climb begins in earnest. Although steep at first, the angle eases later. The trail is clear all the way, much of it through forest, while open stretches afford wonderful views towards the big wall of Kwangde rising above unseen Namche Bazaar.

Immediately before topping the ridge at Thyangboche the path leads through a *kani* (an entrance archway whose interior is covered with Buddhist paintings), and moments later emerges by a stupa with the large gompa, or monastery, nearby. The view upvalley is a revelation. 'It would be difficult to imagine, much more find, a finer site for worship or for contemplation' wrote Tilman. On his way in to Everest in 1953 John Hunt was equally impressed: 'Thyangboche must be one of the most beautiful places in the world' he commented.

THYANGBOCHE (3867m: 12,687ft) is understandably popular. Groups of trekkers and mountaineers fill all available camping spaces, and the few lodges are often full in the main trekking seasons. During the 3-day Mani Rimdu festival, celebrated here at the full moon of October-November, every bed and every tent space will be taken. Should you find accommodation difficult, it would be worth continuing down the trail towards Pangboche for about 10 minutes where you will find several more lodges.

All Everest expeditions pass through Thyangboche, many of

Thyangboche Monastery commands tremendous views of Ama Dablam (right) and Everest (left) seen peering above the Nuptse wall

which receive the blessings of the head lama before making a start on the mountain itself. Visitors are welcome. After passing through an enclosed courtyard, footwear should be removed before entering the richly decorated main hall, or *lha-khang*, where silk banners and ornamental scrolls hang from the ceiling. Sometimes visitors are presented to the head lama at the end of devotions. On such occasions you will be given a white ceremonial scarf by another monk, and this in turn should be offered to the Abbot with a donation concealed within it.

Although it's not the oldest in Khumbu (Pangboche and Thame pre-date Thyangboche) the monastery serves as the spiritual centre of the district and attracts novice monks from all over Khumbu who come here to study Buddhist teachings. A Sherpa Cultural Centre has also been set up nearby. Despite the valley having been settled for nearly 500 years the first Thyangboche Monastery was not founded until 1916 under instruction from the Abbot of Rongbuk on the north side of Everest. In 1934 it was almost completely destroyed by earthquake. A replacement monastery was built soon after to the same design as the original, but in January 1989, less than a year after it had been provided with its own small-scale electricity supply, it was destroyed by fire caused by a suspected electrical fault. The present monastery rose from the ashes of its predecessor, and was paid for by funds raised both locally and internationally.

THYANGBOCHE - PANGBOCHE - PHERICHE
(or DINGBOCHE)

Distance:	10 kilometres (6 miles)
Time:	4-4¹/₂ hours
Start altitude:	3867m (12,687ft)
Low point:	Imja Khola (3780m: 12,402ft)
Descent:	87m (285ft)
High point:	4282m (14,049ft) (or 4343m: 14,249ft)
Height gain:	502m (1647ft) (or 563m: 1847ft)
Accommodation:	Lodges below Thyangboche and at Deboche, Pangboche, Pheriche and Dingboche

Around Thyangboche the lush canopy of vegetation provided by pine trees and rhododendrons, with spiky shrubs of berberis growing low down, makes a contrast of dark foliage against the soaring white mountains. But as you wander up-valley so the landscape takes on a stark, raw kind of beauty, and by the time you've reached Pangboche vegetation will be sparse. At Pheriche both mountain and valley appear almost sterile by comparison with the luxuriant surroundings of Thyangboche.

Pangboche is a two-part village, upper and lower. The upper village boasts the oldest gompa in Khumbu, reckoned to be about 300 years old and dating from the time when Buddhism was introduced to the valley. A nearby stand of juniper trees appeared, according to legend, after a lama tore out his hair and scattered it on the ground.

On this stage you pass below the outstretched arms of Ama Dablam (6856m: 22,493ft), considered by many to be one of the world's most beautiful mountains. During an attempt to climb its North Ridge in 1959, two members of a British expedition disappeared on the final arête. The first ascent (by the South Ridge) was claimed in 1961 by Michael Ward, Mike Gill, Barry Bishop and Wally Romanes, who were all members of a multi-

national scientific expedition organised by Ed Hillary. Ama Dablam's name means 'Mother's Charm Box' from the hanging glacial lump which appears high up on the mountain's face, resembling the dablam, *or charm box worn by Tibetan women.*

The Everest trail slopes down the hill from Thyangboche Monastery through a scoop of hillside among tall, elegant rhododendrons that are magnificent in spring. In about 10 minutes pass several large lodges, and a few minutes later come to **DEBOCHE** (3757m: 12,326ft, *accommodation, refreshments*). The main trail bypasses the few buildings of this village, which include a Buddhist nunnery, and leads through lovely parkland-like scenery. In two places the trail is divided by long mani walls. Then the valley narrows to a gorge and in about 30 minutes from Thyangboche you come to a short suspension bridge over the narrows of the Imja Khola.

Over the bridge the way climbs upvalley, passes a variety of chortens and mani walls, then goes through a kani beyond which there's a narrow cleft in a rocky spur. A few paces after this cleft the trail divides. The left-hand path goes to upper Pangboche, the right-hand option passes more mani walls and chortens, then slopes down to lower **PANGBOCHE** (3901m: 12,799ft, 1¹/₂ hours, *accommodation, refreshments*) where there are several new lodges.

Pangboche is a large village set in a bewildering maze of drystone walls. Stray from the path at your own risk, it's easy to get 'lost' among the walled-in fields! The trail winds through, and on the far side crosses a stream with a water-driven prayer wheel just above the bridge. Beyond the stream there's a final lodge before the trail picks a route along the valley side devoid of habitation for a while. Across the valley Ama Dablam begins to lose its familiar profile.

About 45 minutes from Pangboche the left-hand rockface has been adorned with Buddhist paintings and some highly coloured manis. In another 10 minutes you should reach **SHOMARE**, a yersa with two or three simple lodges. Wandering through alpine scrub, rising ever higher along the valley, the trail then enters a high, broad meadowland. This is **ORSHO** (3 hours, *accommodation, refreshments*), a yak grazing area with a single basic lodge, the last refreshment stop before either Pheriche or Dingboche. Ahead the valley forks. The left-hand branch is that of the Khumbu Khola and the way to Everest, the right-hand valley that of the Imja Khola.

Beyond the meadows a junction of trails is marked by a small mani wall and a large rock on the left with the words Pheriche and Dingboche painted in red letters upon it, with accompanying arrows directing the respective routes. Whether you go to Pheriche or Dingboche will depend on your plans for the next couple of days. Pheriche is the most obvious, as it lines the main trail to Everest Base Camp, but to approach Everest via Dingboche will not add much to the overall trek in respect of time, while spending two nights there will give an opportunity to explore part of the Imja Khola valley. Both villages are high enough to require careful acclimatisation by all who arrive there.

Route to Pheriche:
The Pheriche trail is much less significant than the Dingboche route at this point, although it soon resumes its customary well trodden appearance. It leaves the main path and climbs straight uphill, quite steeply in places, to reach a high point marked by three cairns, manis and a flutter of prayer flags. Beyond this the way eases round the hillside with continuing fine views of the vast Nuptse-Lhotse wall, then the buildings of Pheriche can be seen in the valley ahead. The trail slopes down to the river, crosses a wooden bridge and soon after enters **PHERICHE** (4252m: 13,950ft), a line of lodges, one of which has a useful shop that stocks a surprising variety of goods, and a Trekkers' Aid Post set on the right-hand side of the broad, open Khumbu valley. This is a notoriously cold and windy place, but its outlook along the valley is quite impressive.

It is advisable to spend two nights here to aid acclimatisation. On the next stage of the trek to Lobuche you will be less likely to suffer altitude sickness if you follow this advice. The following section gives some ideas on how to spend this acclimatisation period.

Route to Dingboche:
From the trail junction continue along the main (right-hand) path which slopes down to cross the Khumbu Khola, then begins the climb to Dingboche. Rising up the western bank of the Imja Khola the way enters a wild landscape reminiscent of high moorland overlooked by the Nuptse-Lhotse wall. Cross a low ridge and, about 40 minutes

from the trail junction, Dingboche will be seen ahead, dun-coloured and flat amongst a grid of drystone walls, and dwarfed by the immensity of the mountains behind it.

DINGBOCHE (4343m: 14,249ft) has a number of lodges, most of which are grouped near the upper part of the village. One or two small but pleasant lodges line the trail as you enter. On the left-hand hillside, which divides the valley from that of the Khumbu Khola, two small stupas can be seen, while Ama Dablam rises in unfamiliar shapes to the south-east. The alpenglow on Lhotse is quite magical from the village.

As with Pheriche it will be necessary to spend at least two nights in Dingboche to aid acclimatisation. The classic walk from here is up to Chhukhung and back, details of which are given after the following section.

TIME IN PHERICHE

The Trekkers' Aid Post in Pheriche, built in 1976 and now run by the Himalayan Rescue Association, is manned by volunteer doctors during the main trekking seasons, and a public lecture is given daily on how to avoid mountain sickness. This is well worth attending. Donations are invited to help keep the post in operation.

As for walks from Pheriche, one recommended outing leads up the hillside immediately behind the Trekkers' Aid Post (there are several narrow trails) to gain the crest of a ridge which forms the divide between the Khumbu valley and that of the Imja Khola. A stupa crowns this ridge at about 4412m (14,475ft), with very fine views over both valleys. From the stupa the continuing trail slopes down to **DINGBOCHE** (4343m: 14,249ft, 30 minutes, *accommodation, refreshments*). Either return to Pheriche by the same path or descend on the main trail heading south-west on the right bank of the Imja Khola as far as its junction with the Pheriche, or Everest, trail. Bear sharp right and follow the familiar route back to base. This circuit would make good use of half a day, or a full day if you spend time exploring Dingboche.

A full day's acclimatisation hike towards the upper Khumbu valley is possible by following the high trail that goes upvalley along the slopes of Pokalde to **DUGLHA**, and return down-valley along the standard Pheriche-Lobuche route. To gain the high path take one of several narrow tracks slanting north-westwards up the hillside beyond the Trekkers' Aid Post. Once you gain this upper trail bear left along a broad natural shelf with wonderful views of Taboche and Cholatse (Jobo Lhaptshan) across the flat-bottomed Khumbu valley. The trail leads into the ablation valley below the Khumbu glacier to join the main route. Just beyond this junction an icy torrent draining the Khumbu glacier is bridged, and above that the trekkers' lodges of **DUGLHA** (4593m: 15,069ft, 2 hours, *accommodation, refreshments*) provide an excuse to stop for lunch before returning down-valley on the main trail.

Yet another option is to climb again onto the dividing crest behind Pheriche, and head north along it, going up towards **NANGKARTSHANG GOMPA** (1^1/$_2$-2 hours) on the slopes of Pokalde. Tilman and Houston went up this ridge in 1950 and enjoyed the spectacular mountain panorama, which embraces Makalu, Lhotse, Cho Oyu and Gyachung Kang. 'In this galaxy, which included a host of unnamed peaks' wrote Tilman, 'neither the lesser nor the greater seemed designed for the use of climbers.'

Pokalde (5086m: 19,049ft), which overlooks both Pheriche and Dingboche, is one of the Khumbu's designated 'trekking peaks' and was first climbed from the Kongma La by Wilfred Noyce, Tom Bourdillon and Michael Ward as part of the 1953 Everest expedition's acclimatisation programme.

TIME IN DINGBOCHE

As it will be necessary to spend at least two nights in Dingboche for acclimatisation purposes the following classic walk to the lodges at the yersa of **CHHUKHUNG** is suggested as the ideal way to fill that time. It involves a round-trip of about 9 kilometres (5^1/$_2$ miles), a height gain of 387m (1269ft) and will take about 3-3^1/$_2$ hours, exclusive of rests.

The trail begins in the main part of the village and heads upvalley on the northern side of the Imja Khola stream. The valley is broad and shallow, with Lhotse dominating on the left and Ama Dablam on the

*Seen from the Imja valley above Dingboche, Taboche (or Taweche)
shows an appealing face*

right. At the head of the valley, beyond a wall of terminal moraine,
can be seen Island Peak (Imja Tse, 6189m: 20,305ft), one of the most
popular trekking peaks in the area.

About 20 minutes from Chhukhung you come to a solitary tea-
house not far from Bibre. Groups sometimes camp near here, especially
if they plan to climb Pokalde or cross the Kongma La between
Pokalde and Kongma Tse - the Kongma La being an optional high
route by which to reach Lobuche.

On the stretch between the tea-house and Chhukhung icy streams
emanating from various glaciers have to be crossed. Usually plank
footbridges are placed across them to save jumping ice-sheathed
rocks. **CHHUKHUNG** (4730m: 15,518ft, *accommodation, refreshments*)
consists of several yak herders' huts, drystone walls and a scattering
of lodges beneath the terminal moraine of the Lhotse glacier.

From Chhukhung views are quite stunning. The South Face of
Lhotse soars an astonishing 3770m (12,369ft) above the lodges (its
average angle is 53°), and the great wall that binds it to Nuptse shows

109

itself in a massive sweep of vertical stone. Ama Dablam's North Face is seen full-on across the valley, with an ice-pleated wall seeming to extend from it. Below that ice wall the Chhukhung glacier is born. Down-valley the shapely Taboche rises above Dingboche, while south-westward, range upon range of snow-capped peaks fill the horizon: Kwangde, already seen close-to from Namche, and Karyolaug, Numbur and Khatang that rise to the north of Ringmo far off in Solu district.

From the top of the moraine behind Chhukhung an interesting overview of the valley may be gained, while Island Peak is seen to better effect from this vantage point. Immediately above the lodges to the north is a large bald hill, sometimes known as Chhukhung Ri and shown on the Schneider map as Point 5043m. From its crown a tremendous view shows Makalu to the east, and a clearer prospect of that amazing ice-pleated wall to the south.

Lhotse (8501m: 27,890ft) dominates Dingboche and the whole of the Imja valley. It's the fourth highest mountain in the world, and while its name (meaning South Peak) seems to demote it to a mere appendage of the higher Mount Everest, it is an apt description, for

Ama Dablam (left) and Kangtega (right), seen from above Duglha

it is indeed the southernmost peak of the Everest massif. The first attempt to climb Lhotse was made in the post-monsoon season of 1955 by a multi-national expedition led by the Swiss-American Norman Dyhrenfurth who, with Ernst Senn and the cartographer Erwin Schneider, spent nearly 5 months on a thorough reconnaissance of the area before launching their attack on the North-West Face. Although Dyhrenfurth's expedition failed to reach the summit, the first ascent was made the following year by Ernst Reiss and Fritz Luchsinger of a Swiss expedition led by Albert Eggler. To date only two routes have been made on the mountain, and it remains the least climbed of any 8000m peak.

PHERICHE - DUGLHA - LOBUCHE

Distance:	8 kilometres (5 miles)
Time:	3-4 hours
Start altitude:	4252m (13,950ft)
High point:	Lobuche (4930m: 16,175ft)
Height gain:	678m (2224ft)
Accommodation:	Lodges at Duglha and Lobuche

The Khumbu valley sweeps toward Pheriche between the towering shape of Taboche and insignificant-looking Pokalde, then curves southward. The valley is broad and flat and with poor, stunted vegetation, but as you progress through it, so its character changes. Instead of continuing in a north-westerly direction, it's necessary to veer right and climb north-east towards the Khumbu glacier. The glacier is not properly seen, but the great bulldozed moraines that line it become a prominent feature of the landscape. Some way above Duglha you enter a stony section with Pumori, Lingtren and Khumbutse blocking the valley-head. Along the crest that unites them runs the border with Tibet. All around huge mountains soar in a crescendo of rock, snow and ice. Yet Mount Everest remains elusive despite its close proximity. Effectively hidden by Nuptse's South-West Face, it will not be seen until you climb above Gorak Shep on the next stage.

The Everest trail remains on the east side of the Khumbu Khola, although there may well be several minor streams to cross as you

111

approach the kharka (summer pasture) of Phulong Karpo, with its stone-built hutments. Taboche and Cholatse both look very fine from here, and there's also a good view down-valley towards Ama Dablam.

Shortly after passing Phulong Karpo the trail begins to climb northward to gain the terminal moraines of the Khumbu glacier. In places the gradient is quite steep, and although laden Sherpas may seem to stride by chatting and laughing as they go, you'll probably be battling the altitude with no breath spare for conversation.

About 1½ hours from Pheriche the trail is joined by another on the right - the high route from Dingboche. At this point cross the moraine crest on the left and descend a short way to the Khumbu Khola. A wooden bridge spans this glacial torrent, and the continuing path then climbs to the opposite moraine where the few lodges of **DUGLHA** (4593m: 15,069ft, 1½ hours, *accommodation, refreshments*) are situated.

Above Duglha the route heads up more moraines. A dusty trail, but easy to follow, it eventually tops a ridge characterised by a number of large cairns and mani stones placed there to commemorate Sherpas (and others) who have lost their lives in the mountains. From this ridge views down-valley are stunning. The way now eases considerably, curves round a boulder slope and then enters a very stony region headed by Pumori. Crossing to the western side of this section of the valley the trail provides clear views of the huge face of Nuptse. It's a pleasant stretch, being drawn as you are into the very heartland of the big mountains. Cross one last rise and round a bend, then come to the huddle of lodges at **LOBUCHE** (4930m: 16,175ft) backed by more moraines.

This can be a busy place, with groups camped on the far side of the stream and around the various lodges. In the days leading up to the biennial Everest Marathon lodge space is at a premium. You'll need a good down jacket and sleeping bag to get through a night here in comfort. Once the sun has left the valley temperatures plunge way below freezing. Even sitting inside a crowded lodge can be a bitter experience, especially when a yak-dung stove belches acrid smoke into the room you'll be sleeping in. Don't forget to drink plenty of liquids at this altitude.

For a wider panorama than may be had from Lobuche itself, climb onto the ridge immediately behind it. The alpenglow on Nuptse is tremendous from here, as well as from the lodges below.

Nuptse (7861m: 25,791ft) is the south-west guardian of the Everest massif, a long ridge system with plunging walls. At its most attractive, Nuptse is seen as a huge ice-gemmed spire from Kala Pattar, but this feature is just one of a number of 'tops', the main summit being located farther along the ridge towards Lhotse. It was first climbed by a route on the difficult South Face in 1961, by a British expedition led by Joe Walmsley. Dennis Davis and Tashi Sherpa spearheaded the ascent, and were followed to the top next day by Chris Bonington, Jim Swallow, Les Brown and Ang Pemba. It was the first Himalayan giant to be tackled by such a severe face route - alpine-type difficulties at advanced altitude.

DINGBOCHE - DUGLHA - LOBUCHE

Distance:	9.5 kilometres (6 miles)
Time:	3-4 hours
Start altitude:	4343m (14,249ft)
High point:	Lobuche (4930m: 16,175ft)
Height gain:	587m (1926ft)
Accommodation:	Lodges at Duglha and Lobuche

Trekkers who have spent a couple of nights in Dingboche may be a little concerned at prospects of starting the day by climbing over the ridge behind the village, but it's much easier than at first it appears, and it'll only take about 30 minutes to cross to Pheriche. Thereafter the trail to Lobuche is the same as that described in the previous section.

However, an alternative, high level trail provides an option worth considering, for it not only offers splendid views over the lower Khumbu valley through which most trekkers and mountaineering expeditions travel, but it also saves making an unnecessary descent, whose loss of height would only need to be corrected later.

Route via Pheriche:

The trail to Pheriche begins at the lower end of Dingboche village, behind a small, single-storey lodge. From here a path climbs the hill heading roughly westward to gain a couple of small white-painted stupas. Continue beyond the top stupa and cross the ridge crest from where a splendid view overlooks the Khumbu valley with Pheriche immediately below. The path twists down to it, reaching the village by the Trekkers' Aid Post. Bear right on a clear trail through the valley. The rest of the way to Lobuche is described in the previous section.

High Route to Lobuche via Duglha:

From the upper, or main part, of Dingboche a trail slants up the ridge dividing the Imja and Khumbu valleys. On the western side a variety of paths will be seen. Avoid those that descend to the valley, but instead work around the hillslope heading north-west on a trail that follows a natural hillside terrace. Views to Taboche and Cholatse across the Khumbu valley are very fine, and as you progress along the trail, so the panorama grows more impressive behind. Directly ahead the way to the Cho La can be seen through a steep and narrow glen. Halfway along the trail you go through the hamlet of yak-herders' huts at **DUSA**.

In about $1^{1}/_{2}$ hours from Dingboche the way enters the ablation valley which slopes down the eastern side of the Khumbu glacier, and there joins the normal route from Pheriche. Cross the moraine crest, descend to the glacial torrent and over this climb to the basic lodges of **DUGLHA** (4593m: 15,069ft, *accommodation, refreshments*).

For the continuing route from Duglha to Lobuche ($1^{1}/_{2}$-$2^{1}/_{2}$ hours) see the previous section.

LOBUCHE - GORAK SHEP - KALA PATTAR

Distance:	6 kilometres (4 miles)
Time:	4-4$^{1}/_{2}$ hours
Start altitude:	4930m (16,175ft)
High point:	Kala Pattar (5623m: 18,448ft)
Height gain:	693m (2273ft)
Accommodation:	Lodges at Gorak Shep

The panorama of mountains and glaciers seen from the summit of Kala Pattar is justifiably famous, and includes the only close view of Mount Everest accessible to non-mountaineers on the Nepalese side. In itself, Kala Pattar has no great charisma, and from Gorak Shep appears to be little more
114

*The lower summit of Kala Pattar overlooks the confluence of the
Khangri and Khumbu glaciers*

115

than a big hill at the foot of Pumori. Only when you climb to its crown do you come to realise that this bare hill has a fine craggy ridge and summit of its own. Two summits, in fact.

Provided you are fit and well acclimatised the climb will be a highlight of the Everest trek in more ways than one. But should you be affected by the altitude, sadly this could be a very hard day. It's a long day in any case, for unless you plan to spend a night at Gorak Shep, you'll have to return to Lobuche for accommodation.

Gorak Shep has a few simple lodges, but the difference in elevation between Lobuche and here is noticeable, and the altitude (5184m: 17,008ft) ensures a very cold and uncomfortable stay. Only if you intend to visit the Everest Base Camp site is it worth the experience. Base Camp does not have much to commend it by comparison with Kala Pattar. There are no views of Everest, just a bewildering prospect of the Khumbu Icefall. Not all expeditions in residence at Base Camp welcome the intrusion of trekkers, and the walk to and from it can be hard work over the rubble-strewn glacier. If you're well acclimatised and have sufficient time at your disposal, by all means visit both Base Camp and Kala Pattar from Gorak Shep. But if it's a choice of one or the other, go for Kala Pattar and take plenty of film for your camera.

Departing the lodges at Lobuche cross the stream below and wander into the ablation valley curving leftwards. The path stays on the left-hand side of the valley, beside the unseen Khumbu glacier, then enters a higher, more narrow step. The way now climbs in a succession of steps, one of the steepest sections being the ascent of a frontal of old moraine. Once above this views begin to expand. Later, the trail weaves a devious course among heaps of moraine to cross the Khangri (or Changri) glacier, goes over the glacial torrent and climbs again. Soon after this you round a curve and there below can be seen the few stone huts of Gorak Shep. The path slopes directly down to them.

GORAK SHEP (5184m: 17,008ft, 1¹/₂-2 hours, *accommodation, refreshments*) is an amazing place, just a few simple lodges perched on the rim of a level basin of glacial sand, with a small lake nearby. Tibetan snow cocks chase one another noisily across the sand, leaving their prints behind them. In 1952 the Swiss Everest expedition used this as their Base Camp site. The following year the successful British expedition called it their Lake Camp, choosing instead to have their base on the Khumbu glacier within striking distance of the Icefall.

Even though Everest is very close, it still cannot be seen from Gorak Shep. However, the majestic Nuptse soars above to the east, its great curtains and pelmets of ice dazzling the sunshine. Directly ahead, across the sand, rises Kala Pattar with Pumori (a Tibetan name meaning 'Daughter Peak' which was given by Mallory in 1921 after his own daughter, Clare) forming a pyramid behind it. Mallory was the first mountaineer to gaze into the Khumbu when, in July 1921, he reached a col between Pumori and Lingtren from the Tibetan side, hoping to find a way onto Everest from there.

Kala Pattar has two summits and two ascent routes. Both paths can be clearly seen from Gorak Shep. The left-hand path of ascent wriggles its way to the secondary summit at 5545m (18,192ft) in about 1-1$\frac{1}{2}$ hours; the other trail slants up the eastern flank to gain the higher summit (5623m: 18,448ft) in about 2 hours or so. Neither route is bothered by technical difficulty, and the use of hands is barely necessary except to steady yourself as you pant for breath in the thin air.

Perhaps the best means of attack is to go up the left-hand trail (in truth this is almost straight ahead as you look at the hill from Gorak Shep) to gain the lower summit, marked by a number of slender cairns, then continue along the ridge (take care as it falls away steeply on the left), scrambling over rocks to reach the higher summit. As you progress from one to the other, so more of Mount Everest becomes visible until at last, as you crouch on the spiky top of Kala Pattar amid a flutter of prayer flags, an incredible panorama is spread before you.

Both summits of Kala Pattar provide spectacular views of Everest, its north and west ridges, its formidable South-West Face and, from the higher top, the South Col too. Trekkers well versed in Everest lore will recognise the various features on display and enjoy picking them out. A lightweight pair of binoculars will come into their own here as you scan the great black triangular face with an inevitable plume of snow trailing from its summit. (A short history of Mount Everest is given in Appendix A.)

Everest, of course, is the main focus of attention, but of far greater beauty is the ice cone of Nuptse that, from this viewpoint, appears much higher than its more illustrious neighbour. At the head of the valley other peaks stutter from the frontier ridge: Pumori (immediately above Kala Pattar), Lingtren, Khumbutse, and to the south of that the difficult pass of the Lho La. West of Pumori a vast curving wall contains the Khangri Shar glacier, while views down-valley extend far beyond the bulldozing, rubble-covered Khumbu glacier to a veritable sea of peaks filling every distant horizon with their mystery. In that mountainous sea far-off Ama Dablam has adopted yet another guise. It is an unforgettable, awe-inspiring panorama.

We do not know precisely which point Tilman and Houston reached when they first surveyed the Khumbu side of Everest in November 1950 from their 'subsidiary feature of about 18,000ft to the south of Pumori', but it could not have been the higher summit of Kala Pattar for they were unable to get a view of the South Col. However, they were probably the first men ever to go high on this spur, while Jimmy Roberts and Dawa Tenzing are credited with making the initial ascent and naming it Kala Pattar; a Hindi name meaning 'black rock'.

Route to Everest Base Camp:

Attempting to visit both Kala Pattar and Base Camp in one day would be too much for most trekkers. If you plan to go to the Base Camp site it's advisable to make a day of it from Gorak Shep. The 7-8 kilometre (5 mile) round-trip will take about 5-6 hours of rough-going.

There's not one single location, but most expeditions choose a site close to the Khumbu Icefall at about 5300m (17,388ft). If there's an expedition in residence, or a site being set up, the route to it should not be too difficult to follow. But at certain times of the year it may be somewhat tortuous to find.

The trail begins to the north of Gorak Shep beyond several memorial stones, and soon makes its way onto the Khumbu glacier over shifting moraine. Once in the centre of the glacier locate and follow whatever signs are there - sometimes little more than occasional 'cairns' of yak dung. If you're lucky there'll be porters or yaks moving up to the camp, in which case you can just tuck in and follow them. Note the upthrusting seracs of ice that adorn the glacier.

Everest Base Camp is not the place from which to view the highest mountain on earth. Everything is foreshortened from here, and Everest itself is well hidden. But the chaos of the Khumbu Icefall, spewing from the Western Cwm, makes an ominous choice as the key to the mountain's approach. No wonder more climbers and Sherpas have died whilst trying to work a route through than anywhere else on the mountain.

WAYS OUT

Returning from Lobuche to Namche by the same trail used on the approach is no bad thing. Seen from the opposite direction individual features of the valley, not to mention the mountains themselves, appear quite different. There'll be different light playing on the mountains too, so the scenery takes on a fresh appeal. You can vary your stopping places, visiting other tea-houses and lodges to those used on the upvalley route. You can also make slight variations in those places where the trail temporarily divides; instead of returning through lower Pangboche, for example, you could visit the upper part of the village to see the gompa there.

But there are also various options available by which to make an alternative way back to Namche, as outlined below. The first two are partial diversions, while the crossing of the Cho La gives a completely different route, going by way of the Gokyo (or upper Dudh Kosi) valley.

To Dingboche by the High Route:

Assuming you stayed in Pheriche on the way up and followed the standard valley route, it would be worth returning by way of the high trail that leads from Duglha to Dingboche. (The upward route was given earlier, in the stage Dingboche - Duglha - Lobuche.) By this route allow 2 days to reach Namche Bazaar.

Descend to **DUGLHA** by the standard trail, cross the glacial stream below the lodges and go up and over the moraine crest on the eastern side. Once over this the trail divides. The standard route descends through the ablation valley, while the high trail cuts ahead, climbs above the ablation valley, and round a shoulder of hillside soon picks up a natural terrace that leads south-eastward on the slopes of Pokalde to pass through the hamlet of **DUSA**. Below lies the Khumbu valley, while views to Ama Dablam and Kangtega are soon extended to include dozens of peaks jostling for attention.

Above Pheriche the trail continues over the ridge that divides the valleys of the Imja Khola and Khumbu Khola, then descends to **DINGBOCHE**. Bear right and walk through the village heading down-valley. The trail remains on the right bank of the Imja Khola, crosses the Khumbu Khola and rejoins the main trail just north of the meadowland of **ORSHO**. Follow the now familiar path down-valley to **PANGBOCHE, THYANGBOCHE** and **NAMCHE**.

To Dingboche via the Kongma La:

The Kongma La (5535m: 18,159ft) lies to the north of Pokalde on the ridge linking that peak with Mehra (also known as Kongma Tse), and its crossing makes an interesting and scenic link between the upper Khumbu and Imja valleys; from Lobuche to Dingboche. It's not a technically difficult pass, under good conditions, but the trail is not always easy to follow from the Khumbu side. It's best left to experienced trekkers, or those with a competent guide. A full day will be needed to complete the crossing.

Head down-valley from Lobuche for about 200m. Cross the Khumbu glacier to pick up a vague trail through the ablation valley and then climb scree and broken rocks towards the pass. The approach is rough under foot and involves an ascent of 600m or more (2000ft). The eastern side is very steep, but the way down makes an initial descending traverse leftwards to gain the shore of the highest of several small lakes that lie trapped by the embracing spurs of Kongma Tse and Pokalde.

Below the tarns the way curves right and slopes roughly southward to gain the Imja valley at the huts of **BIBRE**. Here you join the Dingboche-Chhukhung trail and walk down-valley to **DINGBOCHE**. Next day continue along the right bank of the Imja Khola to rejoin the main trail to Namche shortly after crossing the Khumbu Khola.

To Namche via Cho La and Gokyo:

At 5420m (17,782ft) the Cho La provides an increasingly popular route between the upper Khumbu and Dudh Kosi valleys. Perhaps easier to traverse from west to east, the crossing will require 2 days from Lobuche to Gokyo, and trekkers without tents could possibly find there's nowhere to sleep on the approach to the pass, although one may expect a simple lodge or two to be set up at Dzonglha in the near future. (Check before setting out from Lobuche.) So, 2 days will be needed to reach Gokyo, and a further 1$^{1}/_{2}$-2 days should be allowed for the route down to Namche.

This crossing should only be attempted by experienced trekkers, and in good settled weather conditions. Following heavy snowfall, or in poor visibility, plans for the Cho La should be abandoned. In some seasons ice axe and crampons will be needed to tackle the bare ice of the glacier leading to the pass. At other times trekkers cross without any additional aid but a walking stick.

The first day is a short one. Wander down-valley from Lobuche until the trail crosses the glacial stream. Leave the main route here and follow a minor path which traverses the hillside, then curves to the right into the Tshola glen with the Tshola Tsho lake lying below. Remain high, cross the stream that feeds into the lake and climb through the valley to reach the yersa of **DZONGLHA** (4843m: 15,889ft); a good place to camp in readiness for an early start next morning.

Day two begins by climbing to a moraine crest, then follows a vague line of cairns among boulders keeping close to the left-hand rock wall. The way then heads west, still climbing. Get onto the southern edge of the glacier but beware crevasses, and the bergschrund which may, or may not, be bridged with snow.

Once over the pass the descent negotiates a steep slope, sometimes of snow, sometimes bare rock and loose stones. In 3-4 hours from the Cho La the trail leads to a group of simple lodges at **DRAGNAG** (4690m: 15,387ft). Round the corner to the north of the huts a cairn on the moraine wall marks the point where a route heads across the Ngozumpa glacier. Once across this, and over the lateral moraine on the western side, turn right and walk up the ablation valley to gain the growing number of lodges at **GOKYO**. (For full details of this area, refer to the following section.)

Time and energy permitting at least a day should be spent at Gokyo, if only to climb Gokyo Ri (see below). But when it's time to leave, simply follow the main trail down-valley on the right flank. There are several lodges and tea-houses evenly spaced along the path all the way to Namche.

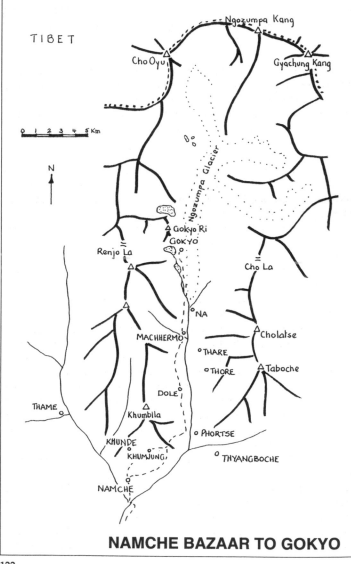

TIBET

Ngozumpa Kang

Cho Oyu

Gyachung Kang

0 1 2 3 4 5 Km

N

Ngozumpa Glacier

Gokyo Ri

GOKYO

Renjo La

Cho La

NA

Cholatse

MACHHERMO

THARE

THORE

Taboche

DOLE

Khumbila

THAME

KHUNDE

PHORTSE

KHUMJUNG

THYANGBOCHE

NAMCHE

NAMCHE BAZAAR TO GOKYO

NAMCHE BAZAAR TO GOKYO

At the head of the Dudh Kosi valley the great white massif of Cho Oyu spawns Nepal's longest glacier. Cho Oyu is a big mountain with a long ridge system spreading to the north-east and the south; its northern side plunges into Tibet, while the Nepalese slopes of tumbling ice face down the valley to a stupendous array of little-known, but fabulously shaped peaks.

East of Cho Oyu, the angular Gyachung Kang is extremely handsome with steep walls and buttresses and clusters of ice. Just to the south of that is the glacial Nup La which leads to Tibet. The international frontier continues in a long curve south-eastwards to Pumori and Everest, but a secondary ridge system breaks away to form the dividing wall between the Dudh Kosi's valley and the Khangri (Changri) glaciers that drain into the Khumbu. This south-forging ridge becomes the eastern wall of the Dudh Kosi, or Gokyo, valley; a wall punctuated by the noble peaks of Cholatse (Jobo Lhaptsham) and Taboche.

The valley's western wall is not as high as its counterpart to the east, but is not without its attractions. Of special beauty here is the Machhermo glen with Kyajo Ri and some fine-looking unnamed peaks at its head. North of Kyajo Ri the 5417m (17,772ft) Renjo Pass provides a link with the Bhote Kosi valley on the west, but special permission is required to enter that valley above Thame.

Draining down the centre of the Dudh Kosi valley the Ngozumpa glacier is covered with rubble and dirty, temporary tarns, but the ablation trough running along its western edge is brightened by a series of lakes, one of which is a deep jade green in colour. By the side of it stand the Gokyo lodges.

Beyond the glacier's snout the Dudh Kosi digs a deep and narrow trench as it bullies its way south before being swollen by the Imja Khola below Thyangboche's wooded spur. Hundreds of metres above the river, trails lead along high corrugated terraces on both sides of the valley. Along the western flank there are lodges, tea-houses and yak pastures. On the eastern side a handful of small villages are set in glorious isolation, at first glance untouched by tourism.

Gokyo, the upper valley of the Dudh Kosi, is a trekker's wonderland.

Careful acclimatisation is essential for safe trekking to Gokyo. Elevation gain can be rapid, for the trekking stages are comparatively short and it's tempting to push on farther than would be good for you. It is very easy to succumb to mountain sickness on this trek, and you

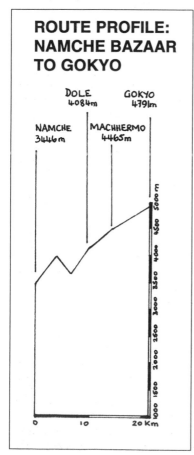

ROUTE PROFILE: NAMCHE BAZAAR TO GOKYO

would be wise to follow advice as given by the Himalayan Rescue Association.

Do not set out from Namche or Khumjung until you've spent at least 3 nights there. If you flew in to Lukla it may well be necessary to spend a further day acclimatising.

Allow a minimum of 3 days to reach Gokyo, spending time in Dole and Machhermo on the way. Inevitably you will arrive at your lodge or campsite early in the day, but it is important that you do not fall to the temptation of pushing on upvalley. Act with patience and prudence and you'll have enough energy to enjoy exploration of the upper valley when you get there.

Lodges are fairly primitive when compared with those at Namche, but will be more than adequate for most trekkers' requirements. In the high season those lodges with a good reputation fill very quickly. Campsites are plentiful and mostly fine.

NAMCHE BAZAAR - DOLE

Distance:	10 kilometres (6¹/₂ miles)
Time:	5-6 hours
Start altitude:	3446m (11,306ft)
Descent:	366m (1201ft)
High point:	Dole (4084m: 13,399ft)
Height gain:	1004m (3294ft)
Accommodation:	Lodges at Kyangjuma, Sanasa, Mong Danda, Phortse Tenga and Dole

As will be noted from the above listing of height gain and loss, this first stage into the Gokyo valley is another switchback. Since Dole is more than 600m higher than Namche, and therefore in excess of the normal recommended daily elevation gain above 3000m, it is doubly important not to leave Namche (or one of the neighbouring villages) until you are suitably acclimatised. Some groups spend a night at Khumjung prior to setting out on the Gokyo trek to take advantage of the extra height of that village. A note of the route from there is given below for those who adopt this plan. An alternative would be to stop early (after 3-3¹/₂ hours) at Phortse Tenga.

Although this is quite a demanding stage, like so many in Khumbu it is a scenically extravagant one. Not only with initial views to Kangtega, Thamserku, Ama Dablam, Nuptse, Lhotse and Everest, but once you make progress through Gokyo's valley, so Cho Oyu makes its presence felt. But there'll be even better things to come beyond Dole.

As you wander along the trail, do take advantage of the tea-houses that are scattered along it. At these altitudes it's necessary to drink plenty of liquids, so the tea-houses are very useful in this respect.

Leave Namche on the classic Everest trail which climbs over the eastern rim of Namche's bowl just above the police check-post. Skirting the headquarters building of Sagarmatha National Park the trail contours gently round the hillside and suddenly presents you with a magnificent view. Everest is seen peering over the ridge linking Nuptse and Lhotse, while Ama Dablam imposes its graceful personality on the whole Khumbu valley.

Now the path hiccups its way along the mountainside high above the Dudh Kosi, and a little over an hour from Namche comes to a small tea-house. Shortly after this you wander through **KYANGJUMA** (3600m: 11,811ft, 1¹/₄ hours, *accommodation, refreshments*), a small settlement with a few lodges lining the trail. Continue ahead for a short distance, sloping downhill among rhododendrons, then cross what appears to be the stony bed of a stream. A few paces beyond this the trail forks.

Take the left-hand, upper trail among trees. This soon climbs steeply above the lodges of **SANASA** (*accommodation, refreshments*), and in about 10 minutes brings you to a major crossing trail (the path from Khumjung - see below). Bear right along it.

Route from Khumjung:

Go down from the village to its eastern end where there is a large chorten (stupa) and a water supply. Just after this, among drystone walls, the trail forks. Take the left-hand option which heads north-eastwards along the slopes of Khumbui Yul Lha and is soon joined by the Namche trail described above. (The alternative trail drops down to join the Namche route at Kyangjuma.)

Now the way becomes a little exposed. Climb a steep flight of steps created up a band of rock, above which the path eases on a steady slanting ascent of open hillside with consistently fine views. This leads directly to a spur of Khumbui Yul Lha upon which there are a few simple lodges, tea-houses and a large chorten; and magnificent views of Ama Dablam, Kangtega and Thamserku, and Thyangboche below and directly across the valley. This is **MONG DANDA** (3973m: 13,035ft, 2¹/₂ hours, *accommodation, refreshments*).

Cross the spur here and descend steeply by way of a series of zig-zags, losing 300m or so of height before coming to the lodges of **PHORTSE TENGA** (3643m: 11,952ft, 3-3¹/₂ hours, *accommodation, refreshments*) near a trail junction. One route crosses the Dudh Kosi in order to reach Phortse, but our trail climbs away from the lodges and passes through light rhododendron woods. About 15 minutes later you come to a National Park check-post, from which you can see Cho Oyu at the head of the valley. From here to Dole will take another 1¹/₂-2 hours.

The route is encouragingly generous, with few steep sections. There are patches of woodland, many streams, a few waterfalls, and steady ascents where height is gained without undue effort. Not long

Mong Danda on the trail to Gokyo

after crossing a small yak pasture with a solitary hut, the trail makes a traverse of hillside, goes over a minor ridge and enters the pastureland of **DOLE** (4084m: 13,399ft) with its handful of lodges and plenty of space for camping.

You'll probably find Dole to be quite a bit colder than Namche, especially when afternoon mists descend on the pastures. You may also be feeling the altitude. If you are suffering any of the symptoms of mild mountain sickness, do not proceed farther upvalley until they have gone. If symptoms persist, or increase in discomfort, return down-valley at least as far as Phortse Tenga where you will hopefully experience an improvement.

DOLE - MACHHERMO

Distance:	4.5 kilometres (3 miles)
Time:	2-2¹/₂ hours
Start altitude:	4084m (13,399ft)
High point:	Machhermo (4465m: 14,649ft)
Height gain:	381m (1250ft)
Accommodation:	Lodges at 'Top Hill', Luza and Machhermo

Prospects of a 2¹/₂ hour, 4.5 kilometre day may not seem very inspiring, but the demands of acclimatisation make this a necessarily short stage. The walk itself is delightful, and as there's such a brief distance to cover there's no need to scurry along the trail. If the weather's in your favour take your time, enjoy the views and let the day take care of itself. However, if you've the energy when you get to Machhermo, you may be tempted to spend some of the day there exploring the magnificent tributary glen that projects behind it. It is one of the finest in all Khumbu.

Beyond the lodges at Dole the trail crosses a stream then swings right to climb round a shoulder of hillside, rising steadily and with the great snowy block of Cho Oyu becoming visible again at the head of the valley. The route crosses an undulating pastureland marked out with drystone walls and with several yak herders' huts dotted around.

In a little under an hour you come to a solitary single-storey lodge (Top Hill Lodge) situated by a large boulder in which a tree is growing. The trail continues past a few more stone-built huts, then makes a fine contour of hillside before descending into a small basin with yet more drystone walls, stone huts and two simple lodges. This is **LUZA** (4390m: 14,403ft, 1 hour 45 minutes, *accommodation, refreshments*).

The path rises out of the northern side of the basin and crosses a high pastureland, the far side of which is marked by a chorten and prayer flags. There are splendid views from here: upvalley, across the valley and back through the valley towards Kangtega. From the chorten you also look down into the tributary glen at whose entrance sit the three lodges of Machhermo. At the head of the glen a spectacular

Everest and Nuptse, the classic view from Kala Pattar
Cho Oyu at the head of Gokyo's valley

Everest, Nuptse, Lhotse and Ama Dablam dominate views
from Thyangboche
The Imja valley between Dingboche and Chhukhung

Machhermo, on the way to Gokyo

rock peak soars above the moraines; on the eastern side of the valley Taboche and Cholatse appear quite majestic, while the Dudh Kosi is blocked at its head by Cho Oyu and Gyachung Kang.

Sloping down into the glen the trail crosses a stream, then rises up a short slope to the yak pastures and lodges of **MACHHERMO** (4465m: 14,649ft). This is a most idyllic site, partially sheltered from the wind by steep spurs of hillside to north and south, and with a tremendous view to the rocky amphitheatre that blocks its glen to the west. Campers can gain additional shelter by pitching their tents beside the stone walls, while tea-house trekkers will find that the lodges here, though basic, are comfortable enough and run by friendly Sherpanis.

Machhermo was the setting for one of Nepal's more believable yeti stories. In 1974 a Sherpa girl was tending her yaks here when a brown-haired yeti knocked her down the slope towards the stream where, no doubt terrified, she watched as her attacker proceeded to break the necks of three yaks by twisting their horns. She reported this to the police who investigated and found tracks - similar to others photographed by Western mountaineers.

This story, oft repeated in various books, was told to me by a sirdar whilst seated in a lodge kitchen in Machhermo. The dancing light of a yak-dung fire threw shadows around the room. The *didi* squatted by the fire preparing a meal and nodded agreement with every sentence of the tale being told. There was no doubting the belief that the Sherpas had in the existence of the yeti, nor of this particular story.

That night I had to leave the warmth of my sleeping bag to attend a call of nature outside - and nervously shone my headtorch into the shadows with every sound that disturbed the frost-still night!

MACHHERMO - GOKYO

Distance:	7 kilometres (4¹/₂ miles)
Time:	3-3¹/₂ hours
Start altitude:	4465m (14,649ft)
High point:	Gokyo (4791m: 15,719ft)
Height gain:	326m (1,070ft)
Accommodation:	Lodges at Pangka and Gokyo

Another short stage, but there are no more lodges beyond Gokyo, and even if you're camping there's no real point in continuing upvalley - at least for a day or so. Gokyo has enough to keep you there, and not only the need to adapt to the altitude. The walk up from Machhermo presents a constantly changing landscape, and the trail under foot varies too. There are broad pastures, narrow clefts with steep-climbing trails, an icy stream to cross, stony wastes and the banks of tarns and lakes to wander by as you progress through an ablation valley beside the Ngozumpa glacier.

Immediately behind the Machhermo lodges the trail to Gokyo climbs round the hillside spur to regain views of Cho Oyu. Now the route makes a steady contour and in about half an hour or so reaches a yersa with a single lodge. This is **PANGKA** (4548m: 14,921ft, *accommodation, refreshments*). From it you gaze directly at the terminal moraine that closes off the end of the Ngozumpa glacier. Keep alongside a drystone wall well to the left of the lodge. At the end of the yersa the trail forks.

Take the right-hand option which slopes down towards the river, then climbs through the ablation valley on the western side of the glacier.

The trail picks its way up among old moraine debris, steeply in places, then crosses a stream by way of a short wooden bridge. Above this the rocks are often glazed with ice as the stream sprays onto the path. Caution is advised. Cairns guide the way up, and emerging from the climb you enter a stony landscape with a small tarn on the left. The valley broadens and the trail meanders easily through, bringing you to a second tarn, much larger than the first.

Beyond this the way eases through a narrow section of ablation valley where a spur of mountain projects from the left, and as you emerge from it so you come to a third lake, jade green in colour and reflecting the white face of Cho Oyu seen ahead. On the eastern shore stands the cluster of lodges of **GOKYO** (4791m: 15,719ft), a wall of moraine rising behind them.

Lodges here are becoming more numerous as the demand from trekkers increases. Some are rather basic and very cold. Others are warmer but smoky. Gokyo Resort Lodge has a greenhouse-style building attached to it that becomes very warm during the day. The same lodge has a small shop with a variety of goods for sale - everything from Cadbury's chocolate (made in India) to hot water bottles and batteries.

TIME IN GOKYO

The assumption is made that you'll spend at least two nights in Gokyo. If you have time it would be worth staying longer for there's plenty to do and to see here. The following suggestions merely hint at the possibilities.

Ngozumpa Glacier Moraine:

The first suggestion is to go up onto the crest of the moraine wall immediately behind the lodges. It will only take a few minutes to reach the top, and once there you have an incredible view across the dirty grey, rubble-strewn Ngozumpa glacier to the great cocked-hat peak of Cholatse (Jobo Lhaptsham 6440m: 21,129ft) and its neighbour,

Cholatse and Taboche wall with Nepal's longest glacier, the Ngozumpa, which flows from Cho Oyu

Taboche (Taweche 6367m: 20,889ft). Views down-valley are equally impressive where Thamserku and Kangtega are once more in view. Upvalley it's Cho Oyu yet again that dominates.

A trail heads north along the very crest and brings you to a viewpoint overlooking a fourth lake. From here you can descend into the ablation valley and walk back through it to Gokyo. This is an easy, short walk that is ideal to help acclimatise to the altitude. It's worth tackling on the afternoon of arrival to help unravel some of the geography of the area.

Upper Lakes & Cho Oyu Base Camp:

Beyond Gokyo several more lakes, of varying sizes, are found on the western side of the glacier. To explore them properly will take a full day at least. If you take a tent and supplies with you it's possible to spend time in the Cho Oyu Base Camp area where there is a cluster of six tarns and some tremendous wild mountain views. If you're fully acclimatised it would still be worth making a visit to them, even if you have to return to the Gokyo lodges the same day. But do carry food and plenty of liquid refreshment with you, plus a first aid kit and warm clothing.

The fourth lake in the valley has already been mentioned as being on view in a short walk along the moraine crest. A fifth lake lies beyond that, about halfway between the fourth lake and Cho Oyu Base Camp. This is also worth a visit in its own right, for a viewpoint above it provides another surprise panorama with Everest drawing your attention. Some reckon it's even better than from either Gokyo Ri or Kala Pattar.

Between the fourth and fifth lakes a scramble up a slope of boulders promises even more extensive views, and will give a good day's exercise. But only if you're well acclimatised.

Ascent of Gokyo Ri (5340m: 17,520ft):

The ascent of Gokyo Ri (or Gokyo Kala Pattar as it's also sometimes known) cannot be recommended too highly. With some justification it is the highlight of most trekkers' visits to the valley, for the panorama its summit affords is classed as one of the truly great Himalayan views, and one that rivals the better known Kala Pattar above Gorak Shep.

An unhindered view of Gyachung Kang (7922m: 25,991ft) is possible from the summit of Gokyo Ri

Gokyo Ri is the obvious hill that rises directly above the lake's northern shore and from the lodges you can clearly see the paths that snake up its southern flanks. There are no technical difficulties in the ascent, but there's a height gain of 549m (1801ft) to face. If you go early (say 7.00am) you stand a good chance of enjoying the summit in wind-free conditions. Afternoon clouds often clothe the mountain, but by sunset they've usually gone. Sunset views are supposedly very fine from the top; but if you plan to experience them, don't forget to take a torch with you to see your way down in the dark.

The path of ascent begins on the far side of the stream that feeds into the lake. At first there are numerous strands to this path, but inevitably they converge towards the summit. This is marked by large cairns and streamers of prayer flags (1¹/₂-3 hours from Gokyo).

A 360° panorama rewards those who get to the top on a clear day. Not only is Mount Everest clearly seen in the east, but also in an outstanding galaxy of peaks are Lhotse, Makalu, Thamserku, Kangtega, Ama Dablam, Cho Oyu, Ngozumpa Kang, Gyachung Kang and many, many more. Far below Gokyo's lake is a turquoise jewel, while the grey glacier has a desolate appearance, the dirty tarns lying upon it making it seem even more so. But above the glacier Cholatse and Taboche make up for that.

Notes on Gokyo's Mountains:

From Cho Oyu to Makalu the range is known as the Mahalungar Himal. It includes four of the world's collection of 8000m (26,247ft) peaks: Cho Oyu, Mount Everest, Lhotse and Makalu.

At the head of the Gokyo valley Cho Oyu (8153m: 26,749ft) is said to be the easiest 8000m peak, in climbing terms, and one that attracted attention almost as soon as Nepal became open. Eric Shipton studied it from the north-west in 1952, and made a half-hearted assault which failed. The Swiss Raymond Lambert led an attempt in 1954, and the same year a small party consisting of the Austrians Tichy and Jochler, with Pasang Dawa Lama, successfully reached the summit. It has since received many ascents and now regularly appears on the list of big peaks being guided by commercial organisations.

Near-neighbour to Cho Oyu is the lovely Gyachung Kang (7922m: 25,991ft). Although it appears quite formidable as it soars above the glaciers, its North-West Ridge provides a surprisingly straightforward route which was climbed by a Japanese expedition in 1964.

Cholatse (6440m: 21,129ft) is shown as Jobo Lhaptshan on the Schneider Khumbu Himal map, although it's hardly ever called by this name. Rising directly above the Cho La it received its first ascent in 1982 by the Anglo-American rope of John Roskelly, Vernon Clevinger, Galen Rowell and Bill O'Connor.

Taboche (or Taweche) has two summits. One is seen from Gokyo Ri (6367m: 20,889ft), the other is hidden behind it, but is the top more easily seen from the east, from Pheriche, Dingboche and Lobuche. This higher summit is measured at 6542m (21,463ft).

WAYS OUT

The route by which you leave Gokyo depends very much on your plans for the next few days. If your trekking is nearly over and you need to get back to Namche fairly soon, your best bet will be to head down-valley on the easy-to-follow west bank trail. If you still have a few days left and wish to visit Thyangboche before leaving Khumbu there's a fine alternative route down the Dudh Kosi valley on the eastern side. But should you plan to visit Kala Pattar or Everest Base Camp region, you have two options: the direct route over the 5420m (17,782ft) Cho La, or the longer but no less enjoyable valley route. These options are outlined below.

To Lobuche via the Cho La:

Crossing the Cho La has already been described in the opposite direction, coming from Lobuche. The trek over from Gokyo is a little easier, but it still remains a demanding route and one that should be left to experienced, acclimatised trekkers under settled weather conditions. The first stage is a half-day walk from Gokyo to Dragnag by way of the Ngozumpa glacier, but the next day is a long one if you intend to reach Lobuche. Groups will sometimes camp long before then. If porters are used they must be adequately equipped for the cold and snow.

Down-valley from Gokyo, between the first and second tarns, a line of cairns heads off to the left to direct the way over the glacier to **DRAGNAG** (4690m: 15,387ft) where there are two simple lodges. It is advisable to spend the night there and make an early start for the pass next morning.

The Cho La is situated to the north-east of Dragnag and is 730m (2395ft) higher. Heading up through pasture and moraines, the way steepens on scree or snow to gain the pass (marked 5420m on the Schneider map, and Chola Col on the Mandala sheet). It's important to remain on the south side of the glacier on the descent from the pass, and leave it in favour of rock as soon as you can. Cairns and traces of path then lead down to the yersa of **DZONGLHA** (4843m: 15,889ft). From there one trail descends directly to **DUGLHA** (4593m: 15,069ft), where there are simple lodges on the main trail between Pheriche and Lobuche (about 2 hours from the latter). Another option is to take a trail that skirts round the mountain spur south-east of Dzonglha, above the Tshola Tsho lake. This is a more direct route to Lobuche.

East Bank Descent of the Gokyo Valley to Phortse:

Instead of returning down-valley along the standard west bank trail, this option is a highly recommended alternative. It provides delightful views unsuspected from the opposite side of the valley and, beyond Phortse, gives a chance to join the standard Everest Base Camp trail, or a different way of reaching Thyangboche. From Gokyo to Phortse is a fairly long stage (6-7 hours), and the trail is exposed in places.

First head south from Gokyo on the standard trail, but after emerging from the steep descent from the ablation valley, instead of climbing up to Pangka, continue down to the river and cross to the left bank on a bridge. Shortly after this come to the tiny hamlet of **NA** (4400m: 14,436ft) where there are two small, very basic lodges. The trail goes through a walled enclosure to a junction of paths. Go straight ahead and descend to a second stream, also crossed by bridge. Over this bear right. The way now passes a yersa, descends to the Dudh Kosi, then winds among small streams and scrub before starting a long rising traverse of the left-hand hillside.

About 45 minutes from Na you come to the scattered buildings of **THARE** (4343m: 14,249ft). This is unnamed on the Schneider map, while the next village (Thore) is misnamed as Thare. Thare has a single tea-house set just below the trail. Beyond it the way crosses a stream then continues an undulating course, coming to a spur with

Tea-house at Thare on the east bank of the Gokyo valley

Phortse, a lovely traditional Sherpa village off the main Everest trail

a magnificent view to the jagged aiguille-like peaks of Khumbui Yul Lha above the west side of the valley.

THORE (4400m: 14,436ft) is reached about half an hour from Thare. This is a small settlement with one simple lodge. The trail continues as a splendid belvedere before dropping into a gully and climbing out again to a ridge topped by a solitary tea-house. Next comes a small pass adorned by a large chorten and lots of prayer flags, with a first view of Phortse way below. Thamserku and Kangtega make a fine backdrop.

Descending steeply the trail crosses a tributary stream by the walled fields of **KONAR**. In a little under an hour from there, having passed through juniper, birch and rhododendron forest, you come to **PHORTSE** (3800m: 12,467ft), a scattered village on a broad slope of hillside tilted to the south above the confluence of the Dudh Kosi and Imja Khola. Phortse is full of unspoilt charm. There are two places to stay: Namaste Lodge and Khumbu Lodge. The first is in the lower part of the village, the second on the upper, eastern edge.

Phortse to Namche, Pangboche or Thyangboche:

From Phortse more options are available. One is to return directly to Namche. Another is to head up the Khumbu towards Everest Base Camp, while a third suggestion is to cross the deep Imja Khola to visit Thyangboche - either to make your way upvalley from there, or to return to Namche along the main valley route.

First, the direct return to Namche. Descend by a forest trail heading north from the lower part of the village. It drops to the Dudh Kosi at **PHORTSE TENGA** where you bear left on the main Namche-Gokyo trail, climbing to the high spur at Mong Danda.

Next, the Everest route to Pangboche. This trail begins at the upper part of the village (not the trail heading round the hillside directly from the Khumbu Lodge). It makes a high belvedere way above the river and is exposed in places. It continues round (beautiful views) to the upper part of **PANGBOCHE** near the gompa. There you join the main trail upvalley on the stage described from Thyangboche to either Pheriche or Dingboche.

Finally, the route to Thyangboche. This begins east of the Khumbu Lodge, contours round the hillside, then becomes rather narrow and exposed before making a steep descent to the Imja Khola. Across the river a steep trail climbs the forested ridge on which **THYANGBOCHE** and its monastery rest (about 2 hours from Phortse). Here you join the main Namche-Everest trail.

Other Trek Ideas

Those treks already described are, quite justifiably, classic routes that explore the best of Solu-Khumbu. But that is not to suggest they are the only ones worth considering, for several others exist, either as major treks in their own right or as variations. Some require mountaineering skills and additional equipment to tackle them. Some are most definitely serious propositions with certain objective dangers to consider. Most are not possible without tents and food being carried, for once you leave the well trodden trails there's a distinct shortage of tea-houses and lodges.

The following route outlines are given merely to draw your attention to the wide potential that exists in the Everest region for further explorations. A number of commercial trekking companies include some of these routes in their brochures, so if your first visit to Solu-Khumbu has inspired you to return for more, you'll find plenty of temptations to join a group.

1) Khumbu from the Arun Valley (Arun to Everest):

When the Houston-Tilman party walked in to Everest in 1950, this is the route they took. The following year Eric Shipton's Everest reconnaissance expedition also approached Khumbu from the Arun valley, but the precedent was almost forgotten in the ensuing years as the march from the Kathmandu valley was seen as being more appropriate. However, trekkers seeking a less-travelled way began to look to the Arun where the route was found to have its own essential character, quite different to that of Solu-Khumbu. At first there were no lodges along the trail, but now there are enough to provide simple (in some cases very simple) accommodation for independent trekkers. Most who tackle the Arun to Everest trail, however, do so under the auspices of an organised group.

There are several options to begin the route. One is to start in the foothill bazaar town of Hille (fine views to Makalu and Chamlang), which is approached from Kathmandu by air to Biratnagar, followed by bus ride via Dharan and Dhankuta. Another option is to fly direct from Kathmandu to Tumlingtar, thus saving two days on the walk from Hille.

North of Tumlingtar the trek leaves the Arun valley and heads west to **PHEDI** with a climb from there to the **SALPA BHANJYANG** (Salpa Pass 3349m: 10,988ft) marked by a large chorten. Over this the trail drops quickly to **SANAM**, and from there to **GUDEL** and **BUNG**. Between Gudel and Bung there's the deep Hongu valley to cross - 'an appallingly deep valley' is how Tilman described it. After a frustrating descent a suspension bridge takes you over the Hongu Khola, beyond which is the steep climb to Bung, a large Rai village set among fertile terraces.

The next pass is the **SURKE LA** (3085m: 10,121ft) giving access to the Hinku valley. Near its head, and separating it from the parallel Hongu valley, is Mera Peak, highest of Nepal's permitted 'trekking peaks'. Across the Hinku Khola the trail climbs again, this time to gain the **SATU LA** (or Pangum La 3173m: 10,410ft) from where you descend to the Dudh Kosi, either at **KHARIKHOLA** or **BUPSA**, there to join the main Everest trek route described in detail elsewhere in this book.

From Hille to Kharikhola will take about 8-9 days; from Tumlingtar about 2 days less. Commercial trekking groups usually allow 20-24 days for the Arun to Everest trek (Kathmandu-Kathmandu), their high point being Kala Pattar before returning to Lukla for the flight out.

2) Makalu Base Camp:

Though not strictly in the immediate Everest region, the world's fifth highest mountain is close enough to warrant mention here. As it shares the initial stages of the Arun to Everest route it's worth including the very fine trek to Makalu Base Camp. This is quite a different proposition to the previously mentioned route; it's not a 'tea-house trek' for a good half of the way is beyond villages and parties must be self-sufficient for a bare minimum of 8 days - considerably more if the plan is to spend time exploring the base camp area.

Beginning either in Hille or Tumlingtar the route follows the Arun river upstream. There is a trail on the west bank, but the more popular option is to climb onto a ridge above the east bank at the district headquarters of **KHANDBARI** and follow it northwards to **NUM**, beyond which the Arun is crossed to its northern side. Now begins a climb to **SEDUA** and the final village of **TASHIGAON**, marking the half-way point; from Tumlingtar it's been 5 days to here, another 5 to go. Until now the altitude has been moderate, but this is about to change.

Above Tashigaon the way climbs to **SHIPTON PASS** - two passes actually, both over 4100m (13,451ft) and with a tarn caught between them - with stunning views on the way to it; views that include Peaks 6 and 7, Chamlang, Makalu and Kanchenjunga. Over the Shipton Pass the descent heads for the valley of the Barun Khola. Once the river has been reached the trek strikes upstream all the way to the base camp site just below the Barun glacier. It's a glorious wild region of big peaks and glaciers, with lots of opportunities for exploration. It's worth allowing time for this.

3) The Hinku and Hongu Valleys:

The valleys of the Hinku and Hongu Kholas are parallel major tributaries of the Dudh Kosi. Rising among glacial mountains east of the main valley they flow south-westward to join the Dudh Kosi some way downstream of Jubing. Near the head of the shorter Hinku valley tower Kusum Kangguru and Mera Peak, while the upper Hongu valley is enclosed by an amphitheatre whose summits include Ama Dablam, Baruntse and Chamlang.

A magnificent, but serious, trek explores the headwaters of both these valleys, with an exit via the tricky pass of Amphu Labtsa (5780m: 18,963ft) to the Imja valley above Chhukhung, thereby enabling a circuit to be completed through the Khumbu. Until fairly recently the high Mingbo La (5817m: 19,085ft) to the south-east of Ama Dablam provided an alternative escape from the Hongu valley, but this has lost much of its former appeal as conditions have changed, turning this crossing into a very dangerous proposition.

The circuit remains a mountaineering route. But well organised parties, properly equipped and self-sufficient for the majority of the trek, will find the isolation of the Hongu basin rich with an austere kind of beauty. An ascent of Mera Peak (6476m: 21,247ft) is often included as part of this tour by several commercial trekking companies.

It should be stressed that this is a serious trek and only experienced parties should consider it. Should the weather turn bad, escape from the Hongu basin can be extremely difficult. Porters must be properly equipped, and if anyone gets sick there's little chance of outside help should an emergency evacuation be necessary.

Most parties fly in to **LUKLA**, then cross the 4580m (15,026ft) **ZATRWALA LA** to gain the valley of the Hinku Khola. It should be obvious that proper acclimatisation is essential before tackling this pass. The route then moves steadily through the Hinku valley, and about 4 days into the trek reaches a beautiful grazing area known as **TANGNAG**, beyond which the trail gets steeper on the way to **KHARE**, situated near the glacier draining from the Mera La.

The **MERA LA** (5415m: 17,766ft) is found to the north of Mera Peak, and is the key to the route into the Hongu valley. Descending from it below Peak 41 the way remains high above the river for a while, with the West Face of Chamlang looming across the valley. Once river-level has been reached the route heads upstream for 2 or 3 days to gain the sacred tarns of Panch Pokhari speckled blue-grey beneath the high cirque breached by the Amphu Labtsa. Crossing the **AMPHU LABTSA** (magnificent views of Lhotse ahead) is the crux of the expedition, but once over this the serious nature of the trek gives way to more gentle walking, first below Island Peak, then down to **CHHUKHUNG**, **DINGBOCHE** and the Khumbu valley.

4) Rolwaling:

To the west of Solu-Khumbu the Rolwaling valley, overlooked by Gaurishankar (7145m: 23,441ft), offers a more remote and wild kind of trekking experience than does the more popular Everest region. Partially explored in 1951 by members of Shipton's Everest reconnaissance expedition, W H Murray returned the following year with a quartet of Scottish mountaineers who concentrated their efforts on some of Rolwaling's peaks and passes. This expedition was described by Tom Weir in his book *East of Kathmandu*. Then in 1955 a small party led by Alf Gregory mapped the area and climbed no less than 19 summits. A number of other climbing expeditions followed, many aiming for Gaurishankar as the big prize, although not exclusively, for several other high peaks provide challenge. Today Rolwaling has two scheduled 'trekking peaks' to aim for: Ramdung and Parchamo.

The valley flows east to west for about 24 kilometres (15 miles) into the Bhote Kosi. In that distance there's a change in height of around 4000m (13,000ft) between the glacial slopes below the Trashi Labtsa, and the point where the Rolwaling Khola enters the Bhote Kosi. The major village is **BEDING**, an attractive settlement that is deserted in winter. There are no real lodges in Rolwaling, although 'tea-house trekkers' should have no undue difficulty finding somewhere to stay in the inhabited part of the valley. Elsewhere, of course, a tent and food supplies for several days will need to be carried. Trekking here is either a there-and-back the same way journey through the valley, a varied return along the Bhote Kosi, or an exciting through-route by way of the **TRASHI LABTSA** pass above **THAME**, a day's walk from Namche Bazaar.

A there-and-back trek might begin either in **BHARABISE** on the Chinese-built highway to Tibet, with the opportunity to visit **BIGU GOMPA**, or in **DOLAKHA**, near Charikot on the Lamosangu-Jiri road. As for the dangerous Trashi Labtsa pass, this provides access with the Khumbu, but is better to cross from east to west, ie. descending into Rolwaling. The Trashi Labtsa (5755m: 18,881ft) is a glacier pass with sections troubled by stonefall, and an icefall that has to be negotiated.

If trekking upvalley strict adherence to an acclimatisation programme is essential to avoid mountain sickness. More than 2 weeks will be required to walk from either Bharabise or Dolakha to a high camp below the Trashi Labtsa, while suitably acclimatised trekkers leaving Khumbu could reach the road in about half that time from Thame. Note that mountaineering skills, plus rope, ice axe, crampons, etc. will be needed to get over the pass.

Officially Rolwaling is closed to trekkers, but armed with a permit to attempt the 'trekking peak' of Ramdung, a trek permit will be issued by the Immigration Office in Kathmandu.

Mount Everest from Tibet

On the north side, in Tibet, [Mount Everest] does indeed stand up proudly and alone, a true monarch among mountains. But it stands in a very sparsely inhabited part of Tibet, and very few people ever go to Tibet. (Sir Francis Younghusband)

Before the forbidden kingdom of Nepal became accessible in the early 1950s all attempts to climb Mount Everest had been conducted from the north. But following invasion by China in 1950, Tibet was effectively sealed off from the outside world. Only belatedly, and well after trekking had become well and truly established in Nepal, did the closed door policy of Chinese-occupied Tibet, strengthened during the Cultural Revolution, begin to ease. In the late 1970s the first commercial groups of tourists were allowed to visit Lhasa, and in 1981 American mountaineer-photographer Galen Rowell led the first trek to Everest Base Camp above the Rongbuk Monastery.

At first only organised groups were allowed to visit Tibet, but in 1984 the country was opened to independent travellers for the first time. Five years later the whole country was abruptly closed due to political disturbances, and when it reopened it was only for approved groups once more. This is not to suggest that only *commercial* treks are allowed, for it is possible to arrange your own private group (a group may be just two people!), although the organisation required is likely to be rather off-putting to anyone who has not already visited this other-worldly land 'beyond the last blue mountain'.

Anyone planning to visit Tibet for trekking purposes should enquire what the current situation is with regard to freedom of travel there. The situation in Tibet is less predictable than Nepal, but in both countries government requirements and restrictions can change overnight with little or no prior warning. Members of a fully organised trek will normally fly to Lhasa and travel to the mountains from there. Many trekkers add a visit to Tibet onto their travels in Nepal, and have a choice of a journey by air or by road. From Kathmandu there are regular flights to Lhasa, while the Kathmandu-Lhasa road link

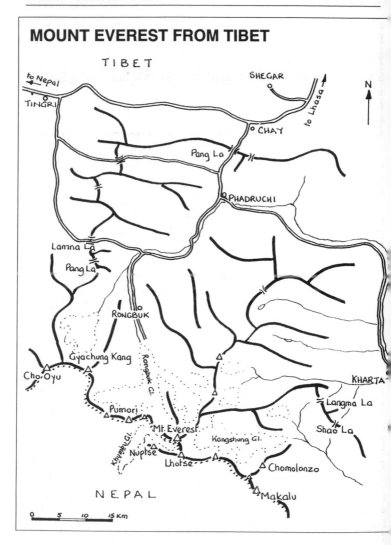

MOUNT EVEREST FROM TIBET

allows a shorter and more direct access to the northern side of Everest.

The North Side of Everest:

Since 1989 all the Tibetan side of the mountain has been included within the Chomolungma Nature Reserve, a huge area that extends far beyond the immediate confines of Mount Everest itself. Under the terms of the agenda for the Nature Reserve programme, not only is wildlife and the natural environment due for protection, but so too is the cultural heritage of the area. In view of the large-scale desecration of monasteries and other symbols of the Buddhist faith that has occurred under Chinese occupation, it will be interesting to see how successfully this ambitious project develops.

The southern boundary of the Chomolungma Nature Reserve is the lofty frontier ridge which, in the immediate Everest area, butts directly against the Sagarmatha National Park of Nepal, thus providing complete protection for the world's highest mountain. On paper, at least.

While it is necessary to climb to the viewpoints of Kala Pattar or Gokyo Ri to see anything more than the summit tip of Everest from the Nepalese side, the mountain's northern aspect is clearly visible far off on the Tibetan plain. And it was, of course, from the north that it was first properly explored - the first seven expeditions approaching through the windblown fastness of Tibet.

From the summit pyramid the West Ridge of Mount Everest slopes down to the Lho La before rising again to Khumbutse, and forms the border between Tibet and Nepal. On the Nepalese side the Khumbu valley stretches south of this ridge, while the great Rongbuk glacier flows northward from it. The North Ridge (Changzheng Ling) projects from the North-East Ridge and effectively separates the Rongbuk from the East Rongbuk glaciers (Rongphu and Dong Rongphu glaciers).

The North-East Ridge terminates at the Rapiu La (Rabu La), a glacier pass of 6548m (21,483ft) which separates the East Rongbuk and Kangshung glaciers. At the head of the Kangshung Face is the South-East Ridge which plunges to the South Col, then rises again to Lhotse. This ridge also carries the Nepal-Tibet border.

On the northern side of the mountain glaciers are much longer than their southern counterparts. But it is by way of the rubble-

147

strewn highway of the East Rongbuk glacier that trekkers in Tibet are able to gain a much broader perspective of the highest mountain on earth than is possible from Nepal. Pressing up to the site of Camp III at the foot of the North Col is, surely, one of the highest (and coldest?) treks in the world.

Three trekking opportunities are outlined below. The first two visit the classic Base Camp site above the Rongbuk Monastery and the third examines the East Face from the Kangshung valley. It is essential to set out on these treks only after a full acclimatisation programme.

Given favourable weather conditions it is possible to trek to the Rongbuk site at any time of the year, but the best trekking season is reckoned to be from May to October, although July to September can be wet. As the Kangshung side is more heavily affected by the monsoon a shorter season applies there: from the middle of May until the end of June, and September to mid-October.

To the Rongbuk Monastery and Base Camp:

There are two main ways of reaching the Base Camp area above Rongbuk Monastery. Both have tracks used by motor vehicles. The first turns off the Kathmandu-Lhasa highway at kilometre 544, a little east of **TINGRI**, less than a day's journey from the Nepalese border. From there it's a 4-day trek to Rongbuk Monastery. There's no accommodation to be had along the way, and the last shop where you can stock up with food is in Tingri. Trekkers must therefore be self-sufficient. The high point along this route is the crossing of the **LAMNA LA** at 5150m (16,896ft).

The other Rongbuk route breaks away from the Kathmandu-Lhasa highway about 12 kilometres (7$^{1}/_{2}$ miles) west of the **SHEGAR** (Xegar) checkpoint, on a track built for the 1960 Chinese Everest expedition. This track actually allows you to drive all the way to the Base Camp site on the edge of the Rongbuk glacier. But that is not trekking! By way of the **PANG LA** (5120m: 16,798ft) a trek of 3-4 days will be needed to reach the Base Camp on foot. Note that there are at least three passes called Pang La in the region. Unlike the above mentioned route from Tingri, this trek now has a number of lodges as far as Rongbuk Monastery.

The rebuilt **RONGBUK MONASTERY** (Dza Rongphu 4980m:

16,339ft) north of the glacier has some accommodation for trekkers, but no food available. The **BASE CAMP** site is a couple of hours beyond, short-cutting the road to it. 'I am not one of those who decry the mountain as unimpressive...' wrote Tilman in 1938. 'Seen from Rongbuk it looms up magnificently, filling the head of the valley. The final pyramid, with or without its streaming banner, is a glorious thing.'

From Base Camp at 5150m (16,896ft) it would be possible for fit, strong and acclimatised trekkers to continue up the East Rongbuk glacier as far as the site of CAMP III below the North Col - familiar from pre-war expedition heroics - at about 6340m (20,801ft).

The Kangshung Valley & East Face Base Camp:

The Kangshung region is much more heavily vegetated than the arid approaches to Rongbuk, and more remote too. From the administrative centre of Kharta a trek of 4-5 days leads to the East Face Base Camp site via the Langma La (5330m: 17,487ft), or in 5-6 days by way of the lower Shao La and the Kaama Tsangpo valley.

KHARTA, above the Phung Chhu or Arun river, is where Howard-Bury, leader of the first Everest reconnaissance expedition, made his base from which to explore the eastern side of the mountain in 1921. It is reached by a spur off the Rongbuk track built for the Chinese Everest expedition mentioned above, the turn-off for Kharta being at Phadruchi.

The **LANGMA LA** is enticingly described by Stephen Venables in his book *Everest: Kangshung Face*. He called it '...the most dramatic I have ever seen'. The trail over the **SHAO LA** (4970m: 16,306ft) is hardly less so, for it leads into what has been called 'one of the most beautiful valleys in the world'. Staggering high mountain scenery, including Everest, Lhotse and Makalu, underlines that beauty. It would be possible, of course, to make a circuit that includes both passes; one on the up-route, the other saved for the return from Base Camp, making a round-trip of about 10 days - plus time to enjoy and explore the Base Camp area. Whatever the choice, trekkers are bound to have a memorable experience. The very stuff of dreams.

To aid these dreams see *Trekking in Tibet* by Gary McCue, and *Tibet: A Trekking Guide to Southern Tibet* by Bob Gibbons and Sian Pritchard-Jones.

Appendices

APPENDIX A: THE STORY OF EVEREST

According to an oft-told story, an official of the Great Trigonometrical Survey of India burst into the office of the Surveyor General one day in 1852 and announced: 'Sir, I have discovered the highest mountain in the world!'

The height of Peak XV, as the mountain was then coded, was calculated as 29,002ft (8840m) - a remarkably near-accurate measurement considering the methods used at the time, and the fact that surveyors had not been allowed into Nepal to further their work. This measurement was generally accepted for over a hundred years until it was increased to the height of 29,028ft (8848m).

Some 13 years after the supremacy of Peak XV had been discovered, it was named Mount Everest in honour of Sir George Everest, the driving force behind the work of the Survey, as Surveyor General from 1830 to 1843. Everest himself was unhappy about such a precedent, being firm in his opinion that mountains should bear the name by which they are locally known. However, despite the fact that the Tibetan name of Chomolungma was known to some members of the Survey, an excuse of ignorance was promoted as both Tibet and Nepal were then off-limits. The name Mount Everest stuck. And so it is known throughout most of the world today.

Although the mountains of Nepal were firmly out of bounds to foreigners until fairly recently, in 1907 an Indian surveyor, Natha Singh, was given permission to map the Dudh Kosi's valley. During his brief visit he managed to go almost to the foot of Everest where he outlined the end of the Khumbu glacier, the first non-Sherpa to venture there.

The first Westerner to gain a reasonable view of the mountain was J.B. Noel who, in 1913, made a clandestine journey into Tibet, specifically to 'seek out the passes that led to Everest and if possible to come to close quarters with the mountain'. He got to within 40 miles (64 kilometres) of it and saw the upper pyramid rising through the shifting clouds. After lecturing on his travels to the Royal Geographical Society in 1919 a committee, formed jointly by the RGS and Alpine Club, began seriously to look at ways of climbing Everest. Little did they realise that their ambition would take more than 30 years to fulfil.

In 1921 the first reconnaissance expedition passed from Sikkim into Tibet and journeyed across the arid, windswept plateau to the base of the mountain. On the way one of the members, Dr A.M. Kellas, died of a heart attack at Kampa Dzong, from where the expedition caught their first sight of the peak. In the party was George Leigh Mallory who, with G.H. Bullock, that year discovered the route to the North Col.

The following year General Bruce led the first proper attempt and, by way of the East Rongbuk glacier and using oxygen, a height of 8320m (27,297ft) was reached on the North-East Ridge. Unfortunately the expedition was blighted when seven Sherpa porters were lost in an avalanche below the North Col.

On the 1924 expedition Lt Col Norton reached 8580m (28,150ft) without the use of supplementary oxygen, but the outcome of this expedition was overshadowed by the disappearance of Mallory and Irvine who were last seen at about 8450m (27,723ft) 'going strong for the top'. Whether they reached the summit will never be known, but that unknown has been the source of much speculation ever since. In 1975 a Chinese climber named Wang Hongbao is said to have found a body at about 8100m (26,575ft). If true this could have been either Mallory or Irvine, but Wang died in an avalanche before anyone had an opportunity to question him closely about it.

A fourth British expedition set out in 1933 under the leadership of Hugh Ruttledge. Once again a height of about 8580m (28,150ft) was reached, and an ice axe found which could have belonged to either Mallory or Irvine. (Several other items of equipment from the 1924 expedition have been found at various times since.) Also in 1933 aerial photographs of Mount Everest were taken as light aircraft flew over the summit for the first time.

The next official expedition had to wait until 1935, but meanwhile an unauthorised solo attempt was made in 1934 by Maurice Wilson, a survivor of Ypres in World War I, who entered Tibet in disguise and, with no more mountaineering background than a few scrambles in the Lake District to his credit, began to climb towards the North Col under the impression that willpower, fasting and faith would see him through. His body was found the following year at a height of 6400m (20,997ft).

The 1935 expedition was led by Eric Shipton, and among the Sherpa porters employed by him was one Tenzing Norgay, the man destined to reach the summit 18 years later. This expedition spent rather too much of its time exploring and mapping, and reached the mountain too late to mount a serious attempt to climb it. Both of the next two expeditions (1936 and '38) were hampered by an early monsoon, and little new was achieved. A year after Tilman's low-key 1938 attempt the world was at war, and more than a decade would pass before another official expedition could be mustered to look seriously at Mount Everest again. By which time Tibet would be out of bounds and mountaineers would need to look at the problem afresh.

But before the Chinese invasion effectively stifled mountaineering activity in Tibet, another clandestine visit was made to Mount Everest by the Canadian Earl Denman. Unlike Wilson, Denman had at least made an effort to learn something of mountaineering at altitude immediately after the war by climbing a number of peaks in East Africa, including Kilimajaro. Of course Kilimajaro and the Virunga mountains were hardly adequate preparation for the highest mountain in the world, and it is no surprise to learn that his attempt failed just below the North Col - despite the fact that of the two Sherpas with him, one was none other than Tenzing Norgay again, for whom 'the pull of Everest was stronger...than any force on earth'.

After the war the forbidden kingdom of Nepal began to relax its closed-door policy at about the same time as Tibet was being invaded by the Chinese communist army. In 1948 a party of Indian scientists were given leave to explore the Bhote Kosi valley, during which they reached the Nangpa La on the borders with Tibet. Two years later Bill Tilman led a small expedition in the region of Manaslu and Annapurna, and before he could return to Britain was invited by the American Oscar Houston to join an informal party that had just received permission to visit Solu-Khumbu. Tilman and Houston's son Charles (with whom he had climbed on Nanda Devi in 1936) pushed up to the head of the Khumbu valley and studied Mount Everest for the first time from the slopes of Kala Pattar. As far as a practicable route to the summit was concerned, Tilman was not impressed by what he saw, and it would be left to his fellow explorer and lightweight expedition guru Eric Shipton to prove that a way did indeed exist into the Western Cwm by way of the Khumbu glacier, and through it would be found the key to the summit.

A remarkable effort was made in 1951 by a forceful Dane, Klavs Becker Larsen, who with a number of Sherpas crossed the Nangpa La into now-forbidden Tibet (the first Westerner to do so) and made his way round to Rongbuk. From there an unauthorised attempt was made to climb Mount Everest by the known route to the North Col. On the way to the col Larsen's Sherpas refused to continue and he was forced to abandon his attempt. Dodging Chinese communist guards out looking for him, he eventually managed to return safely to Nepal.

In the same year that Larsen was making his unorthodox attempt, the British had managed to secure permission to mount a reconnaissance expedition via the Khumbu, and an impressive team under Shipton's leadership made a thorough exploration of the southern approach to Everest, during which they forced a way through the Khumbu Icefall far enough to know that it was possible to enter the Western Cwm. With Shipton were W.H. Murray, Tom Bourdillon, Michael Ward and two New Zealanders, Earle Riddiford and a tall, gangling bee-keeper, Edmund Hillary.

Until now Mount Everest had been very much the preserve of the British, but the government of Nepal broke that monopoly by allowing the Swiss to mount two expeditions in 1952. On both of these Tenzing Norgay was the sirdar. On the pre-monsoon attempt the Swiss broke new ground by climbing through the Western Cwm and reaching the South Col. From a high camp on the col Lambert and Tenzing climbed to about 8595m (28,199ft) on the South-East Ridge before turning back. Later that year, during the post-monsoon attempt, weather conditions prevented movement above the South Col, and although they failed to make any gains on the previous high point, they had at least found a better way to the col itself.

The British were greatly relieved at the Swiss failures for they had booked the mountain for 1953, and in the spring a team of 14 climbers, physiologist, film-maker and reporter from *The Times*, plus 20 Sherpas and 350 porters set up Base Camp at the foot of the Khumbu Icefall.

Leading the expedition was John Hunt, an army officer with five Himalayan expeditions behind him, and an unquestionable flair for organisation. His team was among the strongest ever to be assembled, and included Ed Hillary - who had performed so well with Shipton in 1951 - and the highly experienced sirdar Tenzing Norgay, who by now knew the route to the South Col better than anyone. On 26 May Charles Evans and Tom Bourdillon gained the South Summit (8763m: 28,750ft), a great achievement that is often underplayed in reviews of the mountain's exploration. Three days later Hillary and Tenzing left their Camp IX at about 8504m (27,900ft), crossed the South Summit, battled their way up what has since become known as the Hillary Step, and at 11.30am on 29 May became the first men to stand on the main summit, 101 years after it was discovered to be the highest mountain on earth. In Hillary's words: 'We knocked the bastard off!'

Unknown to organisers of the official '53 expedition, another group of climbers also planned to tackle Everest that year - the Creagh Dhu Club from Scotland. The Creagh Dhu were a tough bunch with little respect for the Establishment, and their idea was to travel out to Nepal as cheaply as they could, trek up to Everest and wherever possible live off stores left behind by the Swiss the previous year, as they tackled the mountain from camp to camp. In the event only John Cunningham and Hamish MacInnes reached Nepal. They had neither sponsorship nor visas, in fact no permission to be in the country at all. When they crossed the border from India they managed to fool officials by showing their passports and an airmail letter bearing an official-looking crest. According to one account they walked through Kathmandu at night to avoid the police, then trekked all the way to Namche Bazaar, hiring a Sherpa who refused to carry any baggage. That left Cunningham and MacInnes with loads of 140lbs each, which they carried porter-style, using head-bands to ease the weight. By the time they reached Gorak Shep Hillary and Tenzing had already climbed the mountain. Cunningham is said to have commented, 'We didn't fancy making the second ascent' so instead they made an attempt on Pumori. Which failed.

Of course, the story of Everest does not end in 1953. In fact the allure of the world's highest mountain seems not to have diminished one iota, for since Hillary and Tenzing's great achievement the momentum has increased by leaps and bounds. Every face and every ridge has been under assault. It has been climbed in winter, climbed without supplementary oxygen, climbed solo. It has been traversed, encircled, skied down, jumped off. In 1988 it was climbed from Base Camp to Summit in 22$^{1/2}$ hours by Frenchman Marc Batard. Climbers have huddled together on the crown and broadcast live television from it. Others have queued for an hour or more at the foot of the Hillary Step, and now Mount Everest even features in the brochures of specialist adventure travel companies - not just as a trek to Base Camp, but a chance to be guided to the very top.

The story of Mount Everest has followed the fate of major peaks in Europe during the Victorian era, when a mountain was first claimed to be 'An inaccessible peak', then 'The most difficult climb in the Alps', then 'An easy day for a lady' (with apologies to women readers).

But perhaps that is unfair. Mount Everest will never quite be an 'easy day' - for ladies or for men. By the original South Col route the technical difficulties may not be as daunting as they once were; the psychology of the unknown has disappeared, and advances in mountaineering technique and equipment have seen to that. But Everest will always be special, if only for the draining effects its great altitude inflicts on those who venture high upon it.

Surely no-one can look upon that great wind-blasted pyramid - from the summit itself, or from the safety of Kala Pattar - without being deeply moved by it.

Everest *is* special, because it is Everest. Chomolungma, 'Goddess Mother of the World'.

For the full story of man's involvement with Mount Everest up to 1989, Walt Unsworth's *Everest* makes compelling reading. But see also other books recommended in the Bibliography.

APPENDIX B: TREKKING PEAKS IN THE SOLU-KHUMBU REGION

The term 'Trekking Peak' is somewhat misleading, for although the summits of such designated mountains are not among the most difficult to scale in the Himalaya, several on the list drawn up by the Nepal Mountaineering Association (NMA) involve serious climbing and are beyond the dreams or abilities of the majority of trekkers. Measuring between 5500 and 6600m (18,045-21,654ft) most of these peaks demand a certain expertise on snow and ice and provide climbing adventure which falls somewhere between alpine and high peak expeditionary mountaineering. The list naturally includes some that prove easier than others, and if tackled under good conditions may seem rather 'tame' to climbers with a few epic alpine experiences behind them. However, in the Himalaya as in the Alps, conditions can vary enormously, and what might be a straightforward 4-day ascent one week can easily turn into a nightmare of life-threatening proportions the next.

Trekking peaks, as opposed to full-scale expedition mountains, are subject to a minimum of formalities and expense, while the rules and regulations governing those who attempt them have been formulated by the NMA. Peaks are grouped according to height. Those of 6000m and above are in Group A, while those under 6000m are listed in Group B. The royalty (climbing fee) for attempting those in Group A is double that for Group B, and is levied on climbing expeditions of up to ten people.

Although there are plenty of foreign and Kathmandu-based trekking companies offering the chance to climb several peaks within the area covered by this guidebook, it is quite feasible to organise your own expedition. A full list of rules and regulations is set out in a booklet available from the NMA at PO Box 1435, Naxal, Hattisar, Kathmandu.

Application is first made to the NMA at the above address. On completion of a form and payment of a modest fee, in foreign currency or in travellers' cheques, a one-month permit is granted. A sirdar, registered by the NMA, must accompany the climbing party for the duration of the trek to and from the peak. The sirdar may also act as a climbing guide.

Those peaks accessible from the Solu-Khumbu region are detailed below. Bill O'Connor's book on *The Trekking Peaks of Nepal* is highly recommended to anyone planning to tackle them. It is widely available in specialist bookshops in the West as well as in those of Kathmandu.

MERA PEAK (6476m: 21,247ft) stands in comparative isolation above the remote Hinku and Hongu valleys to the east of the Dudh Kosi, and is the highest of Nepal's official trekking peaks. It was first climbed by Jimmy Roberts and Sen Tenzing in 1953 while the British were busy on Everest. Views from the summit are extensive and include Everest, Lhotse, Makalu, Chamlang, Kanchenjunga and Cho Oyu. Because of its superior height Mera is one of the most popular trekking peaks, but the difficulties, even of reaching the mountain, should not be underestimated. The shortest route of approach is from Lukla by way of the Zatrwala La (4580m: 15,026ft), but to attempt this crossing without prior acclimatisation is to risk serious AMS. All other access routes, and there are several, have their own difficulties. At least three successful routes have been achieved on the mountain itself. O'Connor lists these as being via the Mera La, the West Face and South-West Pillar. The North Face Glacier route (via Mera La) has also been climbed on ski.

KUSUM KANGGURU (6369m: 20,896ft) teases trekkers on the long walk-in from Jiri. A graceful, multi-summited mountain, it may be seen from several points along the trail, but none better than the brief glimpse it allows between Choplung and Ghat as the way crosses the entrance to the gorge of the Kusum Khola. One glance is sufficient to know that this is a very serious climbing proposition. Kusum Kangguru repelled four attempts to climb it before the first ascent was achieved in 1979 by a Japanese expedition. A number of different routes have subsequently been made. None could be considered easy.

LOBUCHE EAST (6119m: 20,075ft), sometimes spelt Lobuje, rises immediately above the lodges of Lobuche to provide a spectacular panorama of high mountains. Many parties content themselves with reaching a false summit, rather than make a descent into a notch and climbing steep slopes from there to the true top. Few commercial groups attempt the actual summit. The South Ridge route is usually tackled from a camp situated near a small lake reached from the

Duglha to Dzonglha trail, while attempts from the eastern side normally begin with a high camp reached directly from Lobuche's lodges. Note that there is also a separate peak named Lobuche (6145m: 20,161ft) to the north-west of Lobuche East. This is not included on a trekking peak permit.

POKALDE (5806m: 19,049ft) is one of the easiest and most accessible of trekking peaks in the Khumbu. It rises in a rough crested wall above Pheriche, but is usually climbed from a camp sited among a cluster of tarns on the northern side. The Kongma La is just above these tarns and it was from this pass that the mountain was first climbed by members of the successful 1953 Everest expedition as part of their acclimatisation programme.

MEHRA (5820m: 19,094ft), also known as Kongma Tse, is a near-neighbour of Pokalde, from which it is separated by the Kongma La. In fact Mehra and Pokalde form part of Nuptse's South-West Ridge, and as such are well seen from Gorak Shep and Lobuche respectively. Climbing Mehra from the south, groups usually have a base camp at the tarns below the Kongma La at about 5300m (17,388ft), and tackle the peak by way of a glacier which hangs down the southern flank.

ISLAND PEAK (6189m: 20,305ft) was aptly named by Shipton in 1952, although it has since been renamed Imja Tse. As with Pokalde, it also received its first ascent by members of the British Everest expedition of 1953. Island Peak stands near the head of the valley of the Imja Khola beyond Chhukhung and is moated by glaciers. Lhotse soars above it to the north, Baruntse to the south-east, Makalu well to the east. Summit views are magnificent. Not surprisingly it is a very popular trekking peak, although it is not as easy as it appears from below Chhukhung. The narrow North Ridge offers a classic route to the summit, but the South-West Ridge is the one usually taken. In addition to its tremendous summit panorama, Island Peak is also noted for strong winds and avalanche danger, especially following a heavy snowfall.

KWANGDE (6187m: 20,299ft) looks down on Namche Bazaar from its guardian position at the entrance to the Bhote Kosi valley. Many trekkers gain their first view of it from a Namche lodge early in the morning, its upper wall painted by dawn light, its lower reaches still black with night shadow. Also known as Kwange Ri or Kongde, this large mountain has a main ridge 5 kilometres long, and four summits. The highest summit, Kwangde Lho, was reached for the first time in 1975 by a Nepalese expedition. The route used was, like all other routes on the mountain, a serious one.

PARCHAMO (6187m: 20,299ft) overlooks the Trashi Labtsa, the pass which links the Khumbu region with Rolwaling, and actually forms part of the headwall of the Rolwaling valley. Shipton, Gregory and Evans made an attempt on Parchamo from the Trashi Labtsa in 1952, but it was not climbed until three years later when the Merseyside Himalayan expedition swept through the region, claiming no less than 19 summits on the way. The route from the pass is heavily crevassed.

RAMDUNG (5925m: 19,439ft), or Ramdang Go, belongs to the Rolwaling valley, but is included here because of its proximity to the Khumbu. First climbed in 1952 from the Yalung La, a pass to the north of the mountain, the route is over snow and ice slopes that adorn the North-East Face.

APPENDIX C: USEFUL ADDRESSES

1: Selected Overseas Missions of the Nepalese Government:

Embassies:

UK
12a Kensington Palace Gardens
London W8 4QU
(Tel: 0171 229 1594)

USA
2131 Leroy Place
Washington
DC 20008 (Tel: 202 6674550)

France
7 rue de Washington
75008 Paris (Tel: 43592861)

Germany
Im-Hag 15
Bad Godesberg 2
D-5300 Bonn (Tel: 0228 343097)

Consulates:

820 Second Avenue
Suite 202
New York
NY 10017
USA (Tel: 212 3704188)

473 Jackson Street
San Francisco
CA 94111
USA (Tel: 415 4341111)

310 Dupont Street
Toronto
Ontario
Canada (Tel: 416 9687252)

870 Military Road
Suite 1 Strand Centre
Mosman, Sydney
NSW 2088
Australia (Tel: 9603565)

2: Selected Foreign Missions in Nepal:

British Embassy
Lainchaur
Kathmandu (Tel: 411789/410583)

American Embassy
Pani Pokhari
Kathmandu (Tel: 411179/411601)

Australian Embassy
Bhat Bhatani
Kathmandu (Tel: 411578)

The following countries also have Embassies located in Kathmandu:

China: Baluwatar
Germany: Kantipath
Israel: Lazimpat
Japan: Pani Pokhari

France: Lazimpat
India: Lainchaur
Italy: Baluwatar
Korea (North): Patan

Korea (South): Tahachal　　　　　Pakistan: Pani Pokhari
Thailand: Thapathali

The following countries have Kathmandu-based Consulates:

Austria: Kupondole　　　　　　Belgium: Lazimpat
Denmark: Kantipath　　　　　　Finland: Khichpokhari
Netherlands: Kumaripati　　　　Sweden: Khichpokhari
Switzerland: Jawalakhel

In addition the following Cultural Centres are based in Kathmandu:

The British Council　　　　　　French Cultural Centre
Kantipath (Tel: 211305)　　　　Bag Bazar (Tel: 214326)

United States Information Service
New Road (Tel: 211250)

3: Map Suppliers:
Edward Stanford Ltd　　　　　　Bradt Enterprises Inc
12-14 Long Acre　　　　　　　　95 Harvey Street
London　　　　　　　　　　　　Cambridge
WC2E 9LP　　　　　　　　　　　MA 02140 USA

Michael Chessler Books　　　　The Map Shop
PO Box 2436　　　　　　　　　　15 High Street
Evergreen　　　　　　　　　　　Upton-upon-Severn
CO 80439　　　　　　　　　　　Worcs
USA　　　　　　　　　　　　　　(Tel:: 01684 593146)

Note: there are also many booksellers in Kathmandu who stock trekking maps for the Everest region.

4: Health Advice for Travellers:
MASTA (Medical Advisory Service for Travellers Abroad)
Keppel Street
London WC1E 7HT

APPENDIX D: TREKKING AGENCIES

The following list of agents in both Kathmandu and the United Kingdom is not a comprehensive one, but is offered as a guide only. Many other agents exist, and as businesses come and go, and occasionally change their names, some of those actually listed might not survive this edition. Please note that mention of any trekking agent in this book should not be seen as an endorsement of that company's services.

1: Nepal-based Agents:
Note: to telephone Nepal from the UK dial 00 (International code), then 977 + 1 (for Kathmandu) followed by the individual number.

Ang Rita Trek & Expedition
PO Box 7232
Thamel, Kathmandu
(Tel: 226577 Fax: 977 1 229459)

Highland Sherpa Trekking
PO Box 3597
Jyatha Tole, Kathmandu
(Tel: 226487)

Himalayan Explorers
PO Box 1737
Thamel, Kathmandu
(Tel: 226142

Mountain Travel
PO Box 170
Narayan Chour, Naxal
(Tel: 414508)

Mt Kailash Paradise Trekking
PO Box 5343
Kathmandu
(Tel: 475744 Fax: 977 1 471103)

Sherpa Cooperative Trekking
PO Box 1338
Durbar Marg,
Kathmandu
(Tel: 224068

2: Trekking Agents Based in the United Kingdom:

Bufo Ventures
3 Elim Grove
Windermere
(Tel: 015394 45445)

Explore Worldwide
1 Frederick Street
Aldershot
Hants GU11 1LQ (Tel: 01252 344161)

Exodus
9 Weir Road
London SW12 0LT
(Tel: 0181 675 5550)

High Places
Globe Works
Penistone Road
Sheffield S6 3AE (Tel: 0114 2757500)

Karakoram Experience
32 Lake Road
Keswick
Cumbria CA12 5DQ
(Tel: 017687 73966)

Out There Trekking
62 Nettleham Road
Sheffield S8 8SX
(Tel: 0114 2588508)

Roama Travel
Shroton
Blandford
Dorset DT11 8QW
(Tel: 01258 860298)

Specialist Trekking Cooperative
Chapel House
Low Cotehill
Nr Carlisle, Cumbria
(Tel: 01228 562368)

Classic Nepal
33 Metro Avenue
Newton, Derbyshire DE55 5UF
(Tel: 01773 873497)

Explorasia
Sloan Square House
Holbein Place
London SW1W 8NS
(Tel: 0171 973 0482)

Guerba Expeditions
101 Eden Vale Road
Westbury
Wilts BA13 3QX
(Tel: 01373 826611)

Himalayan Kingdoms
20 The Mall
Clifton
Bristol BS8 4DR
(Tel: 0117 9237163)

Nepal Trekking
10 Swinburne Street
Hull HU8 8LY
(Tel: 01482 703135)

Ramblers Holidays
Box 43
Welwyn Garden City
Herts AL8 6PQ
(Tel: 01707 331133)

Sherpa Expeditions
131a Heston Road Road
Hounslow
Middx TW5 0RD
(Tel: 0181 577 7187)

Worldwide Journeys & Expeditions
8 Comeragh Road
London W14 9HP
(Tel: 0171 381 8638)

Although it would be possible to trek the main trails of the Everest region speaking only English, a little effort to communicate with Nepalis in their own language will be amply repaid. If you are travelling with an organised group plenty of opportunities will arise to practise a few words and phrases with your trek crew and porters. Tea-house trekkers will find that some attempt to speak the language will be appreciated by lodge-keepers and owners of tea-houses along the trail, while those who employ a porter-guide will discover that mutual language-exchange is a valuable bonus to the day-to-day pleasures of the trek. Nepalis who meet and work with Europeans are invariably eager to expand their vocabulary, and are usually happy to offer some instruction in their own language in return for help given in English.

The following glossary lists a selection of words that may be useful along the way. However, there are a few Nepali phrasebooks and dictionaries available that would be worth consulting, in addition to Stephen Bezruchka's highly recommended language tape and accompanying book, *Nepali for Trekkers* (The Mountaineers 1991). Lonely Planet publish a small, lightweight *Nepal Phrasebook* that would fit easily into a shirt pocket for instant use on the trail.

aaja .... today
ama .... mother
ava .... father
baato .... trail
baayaan .... left (direction)
banthanti .... the place in the forest
bazaar .... market
bhanjyang .... pass
bhatti .... traditional inn or guest-house
bholi .... tomorrow
Bhot .... Tibet
Bhotyia .... Buddhist people of mountain Nepal
bistaari .... slowly
chang .... home-made beer
charpi .... latrine
chautaara .... trailside platform for resting porters' loads

chaulki .... police post
chini .... sugar
chiso paani .... cold water
chiyaa .... tea
chorpen .... temple guardian
chorten .... Buddhist shrine, like an elaborate cairn
daahine .... right (direction)
daal bhat .... staple meal of Nepal: rice with lentil sauce
danda .... ridge
deurali .... pass on a ridge
dhai .... yoghurt
dhara .... waterspout
dharmsala .... pilgrims' rest house
dokan .... shop (see also pasal)
doko .... porter's conical load-carrying basket
drangka .... stream
dudh .... milk
ghar .... house (see also khangba)
gompa .... Buddhist temple
goth .... herdsman's shelter
hijo .... yesterday
himal .... snow mountain
kang .... mountain
kani .... covered archway, decorated with Buddhist motifs
khaana .... food
khangba .... house (see also ghar)
kharka .... high pasture
khola .... river
khukari .... Gurkha knife with curved blade
kosi .... river
kot .... fortress
la .... high pass
lama .... Buddhist monk or priest
lekh .... hill, or foothill ridge
lho .... south
maasu .... meat
maati baato ...... upper trail
mani .... Buddhist prayer; from the mantra *Om Mani Padme Hum*
mani wall .... stone wall carved with Buddhist mantras
mantra .... religious incantation
momo .... stuffed pastry
namaskar .... more polite form of namaste
namaste .... traditional greeting; it means 'I salute the God within you'

nun .... salt
nup .... west
paani .... water (see also chiso paani, taato paani and umaleko paani)
panchayat .... system of area council
pasal .... shop (see also dokan)
phedi .... literally 'the place at the foot of the hill'
phul .... egg
pokhari .... lake
rakshi .... distilled spirit
ri .... peak
Rimpoche .... reincarnated priest
roti .... bread
sadhu .... Hindu ascetic
satu .... flour
shaligram .... ammonite
shar .... east
Sherpa .... ethnic people of Solu-Khumbu
sherpani .... female Sherpa
sidha .... straight ahead (direction)
sirdar .... man in charge of trek crew
stupa .... large chorten
suntala .... orange (fruit)
taato pani .... hot water
tal .... lake
Thakali .... people of Thak Khola, the upper region of the Kali Gandaki
thanka .... Buddhist scroll painting
thanti .... place
thukpa .... noodle soup
trisul .... trident symbol of followers of Shiva
tsampa .... roasted barley flour
tsho .... lake
ukaalo .... steep uphill
umaleko paani . boiled water
yersa .... a collection of herdsmen's shelters or summer settlement

Days of the Week

Aitobar	Sunday	Bihibaar	Thursday
Sombaar	Monday	Sukrobaar	Friday
Mangalbaar	Tuesday	Sanibaar	Saturday
Budhbaar	Wednesday		

Numbers

1	ek	25	pachhis
2	dui	30	tis
3	tin	35	paitis
4	char	40	chaalis
5	paanch	45	paitaalis
6	chha	50	pachaas
7	saat	55	pachpanna
8	aath	60	saathi
9	nau	65	paisatthi
10	das	70	sattari
11	eghaara	75	pachahattar
12	baahra	80	asi
13	tehra	85	pachaasi
14	chaudha	90	nabbe
15	pandhra	95	panchaanaabbe
16	sohra	100	ek sae
17	satra	1000	ek hajaar
18	athaara		
19	unnaais		
20	bis		

BIBLIOGRAPHY

There is no shortage of books on Nepal, but many of those listed below have specific interest to trekkers concentrating on the Everest region. Several have wider scope, of course, but all contain information relevant to users of this guidebook. Inevitably some are out of print and unobtainable in the West, except through public libraries. But many bookshops in Kathmandu stock an admirable selection of new, old and reprinted volumes, and will be worth investigating if you cannot obtain what you require at home.

1: General Tourist Guides:

The number of general tourist guides to Nepal is growing. Perhaps the best and most comprehensive on the market at present is:
Insight Guide: Nepal edited by Hans Höfer (APA Publications). Expert contributions, both textual and photographic, give this regularly updated book an air of authority.

Others, with similar emphasis on photographic appeal, include The *Insider's Guide to Nepal* by Brian Tetley (Moorland Publishing Co 1991) and *Nepal* (Nelles Guides published by Nelles Verlag/Robertson McCarta 1990).
Nepal: The Rough Guide by David Reed (Rough Guides/Penguin Books 1993) and *Nepal - A Travel Survival Kit* by Tony Wheeler and Richard Everist (Lonely Planet 1990) both offer lots of practical information on getting around Nepal, and include some trekking information.

Not a tourist guide as such, the following large format coffee-table book is packed with an assortment of information and photographs gleaned from the author's wide-ranging travels throughout the country. Toni Hagen was the first man to be given the freedom to explore the whole of Nepal and as such his knowledge of the country must be considered unique. *Nepal: The Kingdom of the Himalayas* by Toni Hagen (Kümmerley and Frey 1980) is highly recommended.

A guidebook to the Sagarmatha National Park, entitled *Mount Everest National Park - Sagarmatha Mother of the Universe* has been produced by Margaret Jefferies, and is published by The Mountaineers (1991).

2: Trekking:

Most trekking guides that focus on Nepal attempt to cover as many areas as possible. Each one contains much of interest and practical use, but for the majority of trekkers whose visit concentrates on one route or one region only, there will inevitably be large passages of unused material contained in them.

Trekking in Nepal by Stephen Bezruchka (Cordee/The Mountaineers - 6th edition 1991) is *the* classic trekker's guide. Packed with information, it is a gem of a book. Sensitively written and regularly revised, the author's love of the country and his concern for the people is a shining example to all who follow in his footsteps. Anyone planning a visit to Nepal should study this book before leaving home.

Trekking in the Nepal Himalaya by Stan Armington (Lonely Planet - 6th edition 1994). A compact guide to five regions of Nepal including, of course, the trek to Everest. The author has spent many years leading trekking parties in the Himalaya and now lives in Kathmandu.

Trekking in Nepal, West Tibet and Bhutan by Hugh Swift (Sierra Club/ Hodder & Stoughton 1989) provides an interesting overview of trekking possibilities in these three countries. It seeks to cover too much territory to give precise detail, but makes enjoyable reading nonetheless.

Trekking in Nepal by Toru Nakano (Springfield Books - latest edition 1990) has a strong photographic content, and some of the illustrations are particularly striking - serves as a reminder to take a camera and plenty of film.

Adventure Treks: Nepal by Bill O'Connor (Crowood Press/Cicerone Press 1990). Not a route guidebook as such, it consists of a series of personal narratives describing various treks, and manages to convey some of the magic - as well as some of the frustrations - of trekking in Nepal.

The Trekking Peaks of Nepal by Bill O'Connor (Crowood Press 1991). This companion volume to *Adventure Treks* is, perhaps, of more value, even if you have no ambition to climb. Brief details of major trekking routes are given, as well as the main purpose of the book, which is to outline possibilities for climbing on all 18 nominated trekking peaks.

Trekking in the Everest Region by Jamie McGuiness (Trailblazer Publications 1993) covers the same area as the present book. Well researched and with lots of background information taking precedence over route details.

Adventure Nepal by Diana Penny Sherpani (Bufo Ventures 1991) is a planning guide for independent trekkers; no detailed route descriptions, but good sound advice throughout.

Trekking in Tibet by Gary McCue (Cordee/The Mountaineers 1991) includes the northern side of Mount Everest. A very informative book and worth having if you consider visiting Tibet.

Tibet: A Trekking Guide to Southern Tibet by Bob Gibbons & Sian Pritchard-Jones (Tiwari's Pilgrims Book House 1993). Published in Kathmandu, this slim guide gives route details for the treks to Everest and Xixapangma.

Classic Walks of the World edited by Walt Unsworth (Oxford Illustrated Press 1985) includes a chapter on the trek from Lukla to Kala Pattar.

3: Mountains & Mountaineering:

There are far too many books that describe expeditions (successful and otherwise) to Mount Everest to be included here, so the list is necessarily selective.

Everest by Walt Unsworth (Oxford Illustrated Press/Grafton Books 1989) is the definitive 'biography' of the mountain. Impeccably researched and intelligently written, the narrative unfolds the story of climbing activity up to 1989. A 'must' for all who have an interest in the world's highest mountain.

Nepal Himalaya by H.W. Tilman (Cambridge University Press 1952 - now contained in the collection of 'The Seven Mountain Travel Books' published by Diadem Books/The Mountaineers 1983). Tilman was the first Westerner to visit the upper Khumbu valley in 1950, and his account of that journey is one of the best sections in this book, which also deals with his travels in Langtang and the Marsyangdi valley east of Annapurna. 'The Seven Mountain Travel Books' collection also contains his *Mount Everest 1938*.

The Ascent of Everest by John Hunt (Hodder & Stoughton 1953). This became an instant classic following the first successful ascent by Hillary and Tenzing in 1953. A new edition appeared in 1993 to mark the 40th anniversary of the climb. All the innocent beauty of Khumbu, as well as the drama of the build-up towards the summit attempt, remain intact. Worth reading.

The Alpine Journal 1993 (Alpine Club/Ernest Press 1993) has a section celebrating the 40th anniversary of the first ascent of Everest, which contains a number of previously unpublished articles and letters of interest to Everest 'buffs'.

Everest: The Best Writing and Pictures by Peter Gillman (Little, Brown 1993) - a superb anthology which contains many little-known gems.

Everest: The West Ridge by Thomas Hornbein (San Francisco 1965, London 1971) tells the story of the American expedition of 1963 that made the first traverse of the mountain and put six members on the summit.

Everest: The Hard Way by Chris Bonington (Hodder & Stoughton 1976). In 1975 Doug Scott and Dougal Haston became the first men to reach the summit via the huge South-West Face, where six previous expeditions had failed. Bonington was the expedition leader.

The Crystal Horizon by Reinhold Messner (Crowood Press 1989). The story of Messner's second oxygenless ascent of Everest, this time solo in 1980, from Tibet.

Everest: Kangshung Face by Stephen Venables (Hodder & Stoughton 1989). In 1988 Venables was part of a four-man expedition attempting to climb the East, or Kangshung, Face which overlooks Tibet. This book recounts the success of that expedition, as well as the horror of descent.

Mount Everest Massif by Jan Kielkowski (Explo Publishers - Gliwice, Poland) - a guidebook describing no less than 124 routes on Everest and its immediate neighbours. No photographs, but scores of line drawings showing routes and attempted routes. Meticulously researched.

4: Travel:

Travels in Nepal by Charlie Pye-Smith (Aurum Press 1988) gives some thought-provoking views on the question of aid to Nepal, as well as being a lively and entertaining travel book. He spends time in Jiri and Namche Bazaar, among others.

Footloose in the Himalaya by Mike Harding (Michael Joseph 1989) is both humorous and thoughtful. Harding describes trekking in Zanskar and Ladakh, in the Annapurna region, and also Namche to Kala

Pattar.

First Across the Roof of the World by Graeme Dingle and Peter Hillary (Hodder & Stoughton 1982). An astonishing tale of a journey on foot from Kanchenjunga to K2 by two New Zealanders and a Sherpa. Some inspiring photographs will set you dreaming about other areas to trek in.

5: Anthropology & Natural History:

Birds of Nepal by Fleming, Fleming and Bangdel (Avalok 1984). A comprehensive field guide, richly illustrated.

A Birdwatcher's Guide to Nepal by Carol Inskipp (Prion 1988).

Concise Flowers of the Himalaya by Oleg Polunin and Adam Stainton (Oxford University Press 1987).

Butterflies of Nepal by Colin Smith (Tecpress 1989).

Wildlife of Nepal by T.K. Shrestha (Tribhuvan University).

People of Nepal by Dor Bahadur Bista (Ratna Pustak Bhandar - 5th edition 1987). Background information on a number of ethnic groups of Nepal.

Sherpas: Reflection on Change in Himalayan Nepal by James F. Fisher (University of California Press 1990).

The Festivals of Nepal by Mary M. Anderson (George Allen & Unwin 1971).

CICERONE GUIDES

Cicerone publish a wide range of reliable guides to walking and climbing in Britain, and other general interest books.

LAKE DISTRICT - General Books
CONISTON COPPER A History
CHRONICLES OF MILNTHORPE
A DREAM OF EDEN -LAKELAND DALES
EDEN TAPESTRY
THE HIGH FELLS OF LAKELAND
LAKELAND - A taste to remember (Recipes)
LAKELAND VILLAGES
LAKELAND TOWNS
THE LAKERS
THE LOST RESORT? (Morecambe)
LOST LANCASHIRE (Furness area)
OUR CUMBRIA Stories of Cumbrian Men and Women
THE PRIORY OF CARTMEL
REFLECTIONS ON THE LAKES
AN ILLUSTRATED COMPANION INTO LAKELAND

LAKE DISTRICT - Guide Books
THE BORDERS OF LAKELAND
BIRDS OF MORECAMBE BAY
CASTLES IN CUMBRIA
CONISTON COPPER MINES Field Guide
THE CUMBRIA CYCLE WAY
THE EDEN WAY
IN SEARCH OF WESTMORLAND
SHORT WALKS IN LAKELND-1: SOUTH LAKELAND
SCRAMBLES IN THE LAKE DISTRICT
MORE SCRAMBLES IN THE LAKE DISTRICT
THE TARNS OF LAKELAND VOL 1 - WEST
WALKING ROUND THE LAKES
WALKS IN SILVERDALE/ARNSIDE
WESTMORLAND HERITAGE WALK
WINTER CLIMBS IN THE LAKE DISTRICT

Northern England (outside the Lakes
BIRDWATCHING ON MERSEYSIDE
CANAL WALKS Vol 1 North
CANOEISTS GUIDE TO THE NORTH EAST
THE CLEVELAND WAY & MISSING LINK
THE DALES WAY
DOUGLAS VALLEY WAY
WALKING IN THE FOREST OF BOWLAND
HADRIANS WALL Vol 1 The Wall Walk
HERITAGE TRAILS IN NW ENGLAND
THE ISLE OF MAN COASTAL PATH
IVORY TOWERS & DRESSED STONES (Follies)
THE LANCASTER CANAL
LANCASTER CANAL WALKS
A WALKERS GUIDE TO THE LANCASTER CANAL
LAUGHS ALONG THE PENNINE WAY
A NORTHERN COAST-TO-COAST
NORTH YORK MOORS Walks
THE REIVERS WAY (Northumberland)
THE RIBBLE WAY
ROCK CLIMBS LANCASHIRE & NW
WALKING DOWN THE LUNE
WALKING IN THE SOUTH PENNINES
WALKING IN THE NORTH PENNINES
WALKING IN THE WOLDS
WALKS IN THE YORKSHIRE DALES (3 VOL)
WALKS IN LANCASHIRE WITCH COUNTRY
WALKS IN THE NORTH YORK MOORS (2 VOL)
WALKS TO YORKSHIRE WATERFALLS (2 vol)
WATERFALL WALKS -TEESDALE & THE HIGH PENNINES
WALKS ON THE WEST PENNINE MOORS
WALKING NORTHERN RAILWAYS (2 vol)
THE YORKSHIRE DALES A walker's guide

Also a full range of EUROPEAN and OVERSEAS guidebooks - walking, long distance trails, scrambling, ice-climbing, rock climbing.

DERBYSHIRE & EAST MIDLANDS
KINDER LOG
HIGH PEAK WALKS
WHITE PEAK WAY
WHITE PEAK WALKS - 2 Vols
WEEKEND WALKS IN THE PEAK DISTRICT
THE VIKING WAY
THE DEVIL'S MILL / WHISTLING CLOUGH (Novels)

WALES & WEST MIDLANDS
ASCENT OF SNOWDON
WALKING IN CHESHIRE
CLWYD ROCK
HEREFORD & THE WYE VALLEY A Walker's Guide
HILLWALKING IN SNOWDONIA
HILL WALKING IN WALES (2 Vols)
THE MOUNTAINS OF ENGLAND & WALES Vol 1 WALES
WALKING OFFA'S DYKE PATH
THE RIDGES OF SNOWDONIA
ROCK CLIMBS IN WEST MIDLANDS
SARN HELEN Walking Roman Road
SCRAMBLES IN SNOWDONIA
SEVERN WALKS
THE SHROPSHIRE HILLS A Walker's Guide
SNOWDONIA WHITE WATER SEA & SURF
WALKING DOWN THE WYE
WELSH WINTER CLIMBS

SOUTH & SOUTH WEST ENGLAND
WALKING IN THE CHILTERNS
COTSWOLD WAY
COTSWOLD WALKS (3 VOLS)
WALKING ON DARTMOOR
WALKERS GUIDE TO DARTMOOR PUBS
EXMOOR & THE QUANTOCKS
THE KENNET & AVON WALK
LONDON THEME WALKS
AN OXBRIDGE WALK
A SOUTHERN COUNTIES BIKE GUIDE
THE SOUTHERN-COAST-TO-COAST
SOUTH DOWNS WAY & DOWNS LINK
SOUTH WEST WAY - 2 Vol
THE TWO MOORS WAY Dartmoor-Exmoor
WALKS IN KENT Bk 2
THE WEALDWAY & VANGUARD WAY

SCOTLAND
THE BORDER COUNTRY - WALKERS GUIDE
BORDER PUBS & INNS A Walker's Guide
CAIRNGORMS WINTER CLIMBS
WALKING THE GALLOWAY HILLS
THE ISLAND OF RHUM
THE SCOTTISH GLENS (Mountainbike Guide)
    Book 1:THE CAIRNGORM GLENS
    Book 2 THE ATHOLL GLENS
    Book 3 THE GLENS OF RANNOCH
SCOTTISH RAILWAY WALKS
SCRAMBLES IN LOCHABER
SCRAMBLES IN SKYE
SKI TOURING IN SCOTLAND
TORRIDON A Walker's Guide
WALKS from the WEST HIGHLAND RAILWAY
WINTER CLIMBS BEN NEVIS & GLENCOE

REGIONAL BOOKS UK & IRELAND
THE ALTERNATIVE PENNINE WAY
CANAL WALKS Vol.1: North
LIMESTONE - 100 BEST CLIMBS
THE PACKHORSE BRIDGES OF ENGLAND
THE RELATIVE HILLS OF BRITAIN
THE MOUNTAINS OF ENGLAND & WALES
    VOL 1 WALES, VOL 2 ENGLAND
THE MOUNTAINS OF IRELAND

Other guides are constantly being added to the Cicerone List.
Available from bookshops, outdoor equipment shops or direct (send s.a.e. for price list) from
CICERONE, 2 POLICE SQUARE, MILNTHORPE, CUMBRIA, LA7 7PY

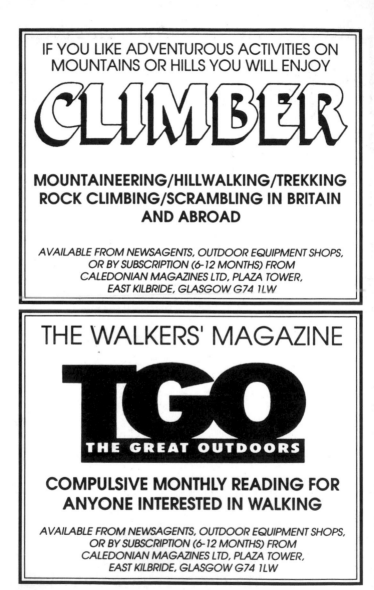
Printed by CARNMOR PRINT & DESIGN
95-97 LONDON ROAD, PRESTON, LANCASHIRE, UK.